Footsteps of Two

Never Give Up: One Mum's Journey
Twins on the Autism Spectrum

Joanne Elaine

Testimonials

What a privilege it was to be a part of the very beginning of this journey. Jo has a lot of energy and has put this energy to good use always, at the heart of all decisions was the best interests of not only Zalie and Flynn but also the whole family. Jo leaves no stone unturned in her efforts to support her kids to be all that they can be – two lucky beings to be so loved unconditionally and celebrated for their differences!!

Jo is one of the most researched families that I have met in all my 30 years in the field of autism. She uses the knowledge gained to be fully informed when making decisions and many of those have been tough ones to make that required her to be selfless in putting aside her own dreams and wishes for her children to ensure that they each had their moments to shine.

A book that will inspire many a parent to keep fighting, to wipe away those tears and use that anger and frustration as momentum to support their kids to be the best that they can be. Autism does not define who you are!

Christine McCulloch
Autism Practitioner

Footsteps of Two is a wonderful and honest journey that provides an insight to one family's experience with autism that is both relatable and unique.

Peter Coleman
Scientist and Marketer

An open and honest account of one mother's journey, navigating nearly two decades of current ASD best practice, with a passionate commitment to securing her children a place in a society where inclusiveness equates to conscious connectedness.

Danuta Bieber

Testimonials

Those people who know Jo will say she is a powerhouse with a big heart and is on the go non-stop. She has a 'never give up' attitude that has made such a difference in the lives of her twins, Zalie and Flynn.

When both were diagnosed with autism, Joanne realised she would be taking a different road, one with many curves and detours and a few bumps along the way. Joanne's personal story of motherhood is a testament to her ability to always look on the bright side, while navigating through the challenges of getting the right support for both the twins' health and different educational needs.

The reader will find this book uplifting as she tells her story about a mum who used her intuition to get an early diagnosis and how meeting the right people to help mentor and support the twins on their journey has led to their personal success. Congratulations.

Vivienne Mason
Publishing Manager and Author

First published by Ultimate World Publishing 2021
Copyright © 2021 Joanne Elaine

ISBN

Paperback: 978-1-922714-16-9
Ebook: 978-1-922714-17-6

Joanne Elaine has asserted her rights under the Copyright, Designs and Patents Act 1988 to be identified as the author of this work. The information in this book is based on the author's experiences and opinions. The publisher specifically disclaims responsibility for any adverse consequences which may result from use of the information contained herein. Permission to use information has been sought by the author. Any breaches will be rectified in further editions of the book.

All rights reserved. No part of this publication may be reproduced, stored in or introduced into a retrieval system, or transmitted in any form, or by any means (electronic, mechanical, photocopying, recording or otherwise) without the prior written permission of the author. Any person who does any unauthorised act in relation to this publication may be liable to criminal prosecution and civil claims for damages. Enquiries should be made through the publisher.

Cover design: Ultimate World Publishing
Layout and typesetting: Ultimate World Publishing
Editor: Isabelle Russell

Ultimate World Publishing
Diamond Creek,
Victoria Australia 3089
www.writeabook.com.au

Note From The Author

Expressions of innocence or guilt are my opinions. These expressions are backed by actual life events.

In telling my story the feelings, emotions, thoughts and memories are their own and they deserve the respect I give them by only writing about them what is necessary in telling my own story. This is my perspective only.

This book may trigger different reactions, and I respect everyone has their own opinion. No one is to be judged for that.

Author's Reflection

I think back to when I was 15 years old and remember a conversation I had with myself: by the time I am 40, I will have travelled the world and have had four children, two boys and two girls.

When you are 15, 40 seems so old. Now that I am 49, thinking back to being 15, if I had my time again, oh, the things I would tell myself. A 'yes' in one situation, or 'no' in another; how your path can change. When you are young, there is always plenty of time, but time moves fast, you realise as you get older. Over 30 years later, I am the proud mum of two boys and two girls and I have seen so many parts of the world.

This is my story, a journey I have travelled over the last 18 years, but I share this story with two very special people: Zalie and Flynn.

Footsteps of two with a third behind: me.

Contents

Note From The Author	vii
Author's Reflection	ix
Introduction	1
Twinkle In My Eye	3
CHAPTER 1: 5-Week Guess	9
CHAPTER 2: Didn't See It Coming	21
CHAPTER 3: Pardon?	35
CHAPTER 4: Climbing A Mountain	45
CHAPTER 5: Trying To Blend In	55
CHAPTER 6: Will Give Anything A Go	69
CHAPTER 7: The School Run	79
CHAPTER 8: Those Moments	93
CHAPTER 9: When Someone Changes Your Life	103
CHAPTER 10: Growing Up	113
CHAPTER 11: On The Road	131
CHAPTER 12: Where Can It Take You?	143
About the Author	153

Introduction

Zalie's engaging smile lights up the room as she stands in the The Barn at Montsalvat. Her latest artwork hangs behind her while photos are taken.

Montsalvat is Australia's oldest continuously active artists' community.

The success and joy that Zalie gets from communicating through her art have enriched her life immensely. Art is a language when the right words are not always easy to find. What you can have trouble explaining verbally can be drawn, painted or sculpted.

At this particular exhibition, Zalie is part of a group of artists who have donated their work for a charity auction.

Flynn, her twin brother, wanders around the beautiful space, proudly sharing a photo or two with his sister. Flynn expresses his own creative side by making furniture, sculpting with tin and drawing.

Our road has taken a different path. When we got in the car and started driving, it was not the cruising coastal route we had planned. We ended up being blocked by a detour sign, having to take the back way through the mountains, wondering if our journey would ever lead us to our desired destination.

I am very proud to be the mum of two unique, kind individuals who I hope will one day be the drivers of their own vehicles on life's road.

So, please, feel free to jump in the back seat with us and come along for the ride.

Twinkle In My Eye

I recall celebrating my 30th birthday at an idyllic restaurant in Kangaroo Ground, Melbourne – a Sunday lunch with about 30 of my family and friends. A gorgeous panoramic view, out the expansive floor to ceiling windows, across to the mountains. My son, Bryce, then 14 months old, sitting on my knee, already chatty at such a young age.

A lovely day to celebrate a milestone in life. With my husband, Matt, we were a small family of three.

I was working part-time at that stage, we had our two pet dogs, Shelties, and were living happily in a leafy suburb of Melbourne. We were in our second home that we had owned in Hurstbridge, having left a small 12-square-metre property we renovated to purchase something larger prior to Bryce being born.

Hurstbridge is a lovely town, with a fantastic local community. We really enjoyed living there.

I got my first taste of organically grown food, swapping the supermarket for the local organic fruit and vegetable shop, and have never looked back. Trying to be a good mum, as you do. Eating organically meant fewer chemicals in and on the food, the taste was far superior and Bryce was an excellent eater – there was nothing he would not try.

My grandparents lived not far up the road in Yarrambat on five acres. They had been there for 50 years.

Bryce loved going to visit Ma and Pa, as we called them. There were cows in the paddock, an aviary of birds, a crazy pet cockatoo, lemons to be picked and a dam to walk around and look for yabbies.

I have always been an active person and walking with the pram kept me fit around the local streets and pushing a pram up a hill is great exercise, while walking the dogs. My mum would look after Bryce two days a week. While I worked, Bryce attended a play group, did swimming lessons and went to gym classes.

Like many young mums these days, I kept social and gave Bryce, then an only child, plenty of social interaction with other kids his age through the activities he did or that we did together.

In the same year of my 30th birthday, Matt and I thought it might be nice to give Bryce a younger brother or sister. At that time, I was seeing a local Bowen therapist, Rosie.

Rosie was a lovely lady in her early seventies and we would have some great laughs and chats during therapy.

Bowen therapy works on the soft connective tissue in the body. It provides great relief for sore shoulders, neck, legs and muscles after exercising. It helps promote a feeling of calm and relaxation, which allows the body to heal and repair. Due to my work commitments at that time and love of exercise, I really enjoyed my Bowen therapy sessions. Often after seeing Rosie in the evening, I would sleep like a baby that night.

Bryce had been conceived quite quickly, so when it came to wanting more children, I honestly thought that it wouldn't be a problem, that things would go like clockwork again and I would be pregnant in no time. This is not always the case, and it wasn't for me.

After trying for many months, I was in a Bowen therapy session one evening, venting to Rosie, chatting about the current goings-on. Sometimes in life it is good to chat to those not immediately close to you to get something that is on your mind out and chat about it to get a different opinion or perspective on a situation.

So, Rosie was happy to listen while I talked about wanting to give Bryce a younger sibling and how it was taking longer to fall pregnant than I thought it would. She said I can help with that. 'Really?' I asked, surprised, as I looked at her. 'How?' As part of my Bowen therapy that day, Rosie also did a quick muscle manipulation just below my hip, and off I went, feeling calm and relaxed as I always did.

I am a very open-minded person when it comes to natural and holistic therapies, happy to give anything a try, as I am a strong believer in these therapies more than traditional medicine. In my younger days I had wanted to be a naturopath and even seriously considered going back to study not long after Bryce was born. I didn't at the time, thinking I had a young family and a good job (then working as an executive assistant at a local hospital). Financially, going back to study could be a burden, so I continued working instead.

It was not even a month after that Bowen therapy session that I found out I was pregnant.

Now, believe what you will – was it psychological? Did I think Rosie had helped me so I relaxed and fell pregnant or did the Bowen therapy actually work? Personally, I think it was the Bowen therapy, as Rosie was a very clever and gifted woman, very in tune with the human body. So, wow, there you go, I was pregnant and looking forward to being a mum again.

As always in the very early stages of pregnancy, you are super cautious. Anything can happen and you need to take it easy. However, it was also at this time, just prior to finding out that I was pregnant, that Matt and I had decided we were going to sell our house. We loved living in Hurstbridge but wanted to move a little closer towards the city, for more options in regards to future schooling and access to things for Bryce. Matt was working in real estate at the time and the housing market was steady. It was a good time to sell. We had only been in our current home for three years but had now decided to make a move. Suddenly, not only was our house on the market, but I had just found out I was pregnant.

We made a wish and two came true.

CHAPTER 1

5-Week Guess

Every woman is different, as are our pregnancy journeys. When I was carrying Bryce, I felt unwell, with a feeling of nausea in the earliest stages of pregnancy from about eight weeks through till 11-12 weeks. That you were going to be sick, but never were. Toothpaste made my stomach turn, as did many foods. I would stop at the local milk bar on my way to work every morning and buy a Lucozade drink, which seemed to settle the stomach and help me to get through the day.

By the end of my first trimester, I was fine. I could eat whatever I wanted, exercise, go to work and my everyday life carried on as usual. Cravings were not extreme: just some potato cakes in the afternoon on my workdays always helped.

So, in my mind, I expected to travel a similar road with my second pregnancy. I was the same weight as I had always been since the age of 14, would you believe, around 48-50 kg, which in my eyes is a bit too skinny for my frame. However, when you are a person with a fast metabolism, putting on weight is not easy – a problem some wish they had. Part of me enjoyed being pregnant, as I got to see myself carrying extra weight and looking healthier.

At about five weeks, I started to feel unwell; just a little nausea in the tummy. I actually was not sure it could be pregnancy-related at that stage. I had not even been to the doctor, so I was really questioning why I didn't feel quite right. At around the same time, I had come across an article in a magazine that mentioned that if you are carrying more than one baby, often you can feel unwell early in the pregnancy. At the time, I dismissed this quickly, however the thought remained in the back of my mind.

My grandparents had raised four children: a son, a daughter and a set of twin boys. There were twins in our family everywhere. Between my cousins and I, we knew the chances of one of us having twins was a strong possibility: my grandfather's sisters were twins, my uncles were twins. My husband's uncles were twins. I had also read that twins skip a generation. So, as my grandmother had twins and none of her children did, myself and my cousins were likely to.

A few days later, I made an appointment with my local GP who confirmed I was pregnant and referred me back to my obstetrician, Dr B. I was then sent for an ultrasound.

5-Week Guess

Well, yes, you guessed it. My five-week thought was correct. I was slightly unwell and it was confirmed I was carrying not one, but two babies.

I will never forget the phone calls I made, first to Matt, then my mum, but the one that sticks in my mind was to my dad. He was a Royal Automobile Club of Victoria (RACV) patrol man at the time. I rang him with Mum standing next to me and it was fairly straightforward. 'Hi, Dad, guess what? I am pregnant,' I said. His response, 'Oh, Joanne, that is wonderful news, congratulations!' 'Dad, I am having twins.' 'What? What did you say?' I replied, 'Dad, I am having twins!' He exclaimed, 'Oh gosh, ring your grandmother.' That was my next phone call.

Well, I think, Ma (as we called her) was the most excited, she was so happy. I remember her yelling out to Pa while on the phone, 'Bill, Bill, Joanne is having twins!' I always felt a special connection to my grandmother and now maybe more so.

It was still early days, at seven weeks, so I did my best to keep it low key, and really did not tell many people. To be honest at the time, other than feeling a little nausea I seemed OK, so I tried to keep my mind on other things, which at that point was looking for a new home.

While finding out I was pregnant with twins, in literally the same week as we sold our house. It had only been on the market a couple of weeks, and it all happened very quickly. Wow! No turning back now.

Matt and I are very house-proud people, so when we sell a home there has always been a lot of hard work that has gone into renovating. At times, there is a sense of loss: 'Oh gosh, we just sold a beautiful home. Yes, of course we have done the right thing...' Lots of hesitation and questioning ourselves! Did we ask for enough money? What now? Will we find something else? Furthermore, the new owners wanted a shorter settlement of only 60 days, which we had agreed to.

As Matt was working in real estate, he was often working on weekends and did not have Saturdays free to go to home inspections, so this was predominantly left up to me. When I found a home I liked, the plan was to then get him around to have a look also.

With about 30 days left until we had to be out of our current home, with plans to stay with my parents in the interim until we found a new place, I attended a house inspection. The home was being auctioned that day – a four-bedroom home in the Woodridge Estate of Eltham. My mum and Bryce had also come along to have a look at this house. It was our last inspection on that particular Saturday.

The home was well built, a bit of a renovator's delight and the layout was good, so Mum and I thought we would stick around to see what price it got at auction.

It came to the end of the auction – well, what seemed to be the end – and the two bidders had slowed and not much was happening, I could see that this house was about to sell at either a ridiculously low price or not at all. Craziness kicked in – a pregnant mum with twins not wanting to move house twice, hoping for a line-up of settlement dates – and I put my hand up at the last minute and bought the house.

5-Week Guess

Without Matt having looked at it, or anyone else other than me and mum and Bryce, who was not even two years old. Suddenly, I was being whisked inside by the real estate agent and I was ringing Matt frantically before sitting down to negotiate with the owner. My mum was there sitting in the car with Bryce, somewhat in shock but also encouraging me with, 'Yes you have made the right decision.'

Matt was beside himself on the other end of the phone, I simply rang him and said I have bought a house in Eltham, just now at auction, that this is the price I am offering and I am aiming to get the same settlement date, so we can move straight out of our Hurstbridge home and into Eltham in 30 days' time. Goodness, what could he say in response to that? Well, the owner accepted my offer and after a bit of deliberation with her family, the 30-day (very short) settlement was also accepted. I must confess, I did throw in the line of being pregnant with twins to help convince her to give us such a short settlement. It worked. It had been her family home and as her husband had passed away, she was keen to move on.

I managed to get Matt to look at the home in the next few days, but the offer was already in and there was no cooling off now. He saw the potential, as did I, and there was a great pre-school for Bryce within walking distance, as well as being able to walk to the local shops. Hopefully, although made hastily, it was the right decision.

So, in less than 30 days we were moving. By that stage, I would be just in my second trimester of pregnancy, all going well.

Bryce was such a bright boy. You could have a full conversation with him, as he could string together structured sentences at

18 months of age. His understanding we were moving house and taking our two dogs from Hurstbridge to Eltham, was very easy to communicate.

On a sunny winter's day in August 2002, we moved house. It was more exhausting than usual due to my pregnancy, finding the right place for everything, filling the kitchen cupboards. My mum, like me, went a bit too hard and by the end of the day, she felt very lightheaded, on the verge of fainting on the couch. But we were in.

We had no plans to renovate straight away, just to relax and assess what needed to be done and prioritise decisions, and for me to rest and look after our babies.

Anyone who knows me also knows my car number plate: GOJOGO. I am always busy, on the move, planning something, never sitting down and putting my feet up on the couch as resting is not something I tend to do. Then, by the end of the day, dinner is done, the washing is folded, the house is tidy, and I might find the time to sit down and watch a bit of TV before I crash and fall asleep. The afternoon naps on the couch as advised for any pregnant mum, were really something I had to make myself do.

Now, with my first pregnancy, I was only unwell till about eight weeks. So, logic was telling me, this time I may actually feel unwell till about 16 weeks. I had to keep reminding myself, and more so my obstetrician had to, that I had two babies in my tummy this time; it is going to be different, it is going to be harder. Rest, rest, rest – which I had been doing, however the demands on my very low body weight to keep myself well-nourished, as well as the twins, was something I was going to have to work hard on.

5-Week Guess

I had a blood test between 9 to 12 weeks and an ultrasound at 12 to 13 weeks, combined these tests told me the risk to my babies of any chromosome defects was that of a mother pregnant in her early twenties and as I was in my early thirties, this was reassuring.

I was close, by the time 16 weeks came around, the daily feeling of an unsettled tummy, slight nausea had subsided, and I was feeling good. I hoped now to enjoy my pregnancy, butterfly flutters and quickly expanding tummy.

As it had been on my mind for a few weeks, I had decided to find out the sex of my babies if I was able to at the 18-week scan. Undergoing many tests and choices in the early stages of pregnancy can at times be overwhelming. I had already been told – I am not sure how they know this – that I had dropped two eggs from my left ovary which was how the twins were conceived.

This meant my twins were fraternal, but the sex still had to be determined and, while nothing is 100 per cent certain at this stage, they could give a good indication. It was by accident that I had sighted the sex of my first born at the 18-week scan, but this time I was actually going to request to know, which was very exciting. I was really hoping for a girl, so I was very pleased when I was told I was having both a boy and a girl.

So pleased, I started to cry happy tears. As they were fraternal twins, they would look like brother and sister, not identical, as many people visualise twins to be. There were apparently fraternal twins in my family several generations back.

In my eyes, knowing the sex of my twins would hopefully help me plan things better, such as their bedrooms, clothing, etc. I also became a bit more relaxed and felt I could now relate to my babies as individuals. They were able to tell me which baby was sitting higher in my tummy at particular stages, I could then chat to them personally and gave them nicknames over the duration of my pregnancy. B1 was my girl and B2 my boy. B2 sat higher and B1 below, so we always said my boy was squashing my girl; she would be the fighter!

It was also at this time that I had the 18 to 20-week scan, also known as the morphology scan, that looks for abnormalities in your baby's structural development and growth, such as spina bifida, the absence of limbs or a cleft palate. It was very reassuring at this point to be advised that both my babies were developing well, and there were no physical signs of any abnormalities.

As the weeks progressed, anyone who saw me said I was the size of some pregnant mothers who were carrying only one baby. I tried to take this as a compliment externally, however internally it definitely did not feel that way. The pressure on the bladder, the difficulty in finding a comfortable sleeping position were all relevant to two babies demanding all they could from me. I did crave different foods and have always been a healthy eater, but cooked prawns and seafood sauce, basically a seafood cocktail on iceberg lettuce, was one of my strongest desires.

I really don't know why and I was very conscious that shellfish and deli foods are not advised during pregnancy, but this is what my body was really enjoying, so I went with it for the few weeks that my body craved it. I also developed a taste for seaweed, which is high in iodine, so could only be beneficial for my twins. Gherkins and potato cakes were other foods I enjoyed. The tang of the gherkins and the saltiness of the potato cakes.

I have always assumed that what you crave in pregnancy is a reflection of what your body is lacking to support your growing baby or babies.

Moving into my third trimester, other than feeling very large, I was well, so it came as a complete shock when, suddenly, at 30 weeks, I could not keep any food down. I was trying my best to relax, eating well. My nausea had settled long ago, however this was really terrible – this was more than nausea. I became very unwell very quickly. Propped up in bed, with Bryce patting my forehead, asking, 'Mum are you OK? I look after you,' he was saying. But I could not hold down any food or liquid.

The last thing I recall trying was a lovely plump red strawberry, which looked so tasty. Nope up that came too. After less than 48 hours, I became quite tired, frustrated and weak. We called my obstetrician and she was very concerned. Dr B was a wonderful obstetrician, a strong-willed woman who spoke very directly and told it as it was. She promptly told Matt off for letting me get in this state and yelled at him for not contacting her sooner. So, at 30 weeks gestation, I was rushed to hospital and treated for dehydration being placed on an intravenous line for 24 hours. I did not have a virus; this was simply my body reacting to trying to feed two babies and myself.

After 24 hours of rehydration and rest in hospital, I felt much better and slowly introduced foods again that I could keep down.

From then on, it was only a few days later that I started to feel well again. All nausea was gone, I had energy back to care for Bryce and resume normal activities.

Other than the time I was admitted to hospital for dehydration, my pregnancy ran very smoothly.

As we neared the end of my third trimester, my obstetrician suggested to me that although my first born was a natural birth, due to my small stature she suggested a caesarean section so there would be less distress to the babies upon birth. She felt I would struggle to push out two babies due to the size of my hips and a long labour would be difficult for both myself and my babies.

After some consideration, I agreed, and the decision was made to take them out at 37-and-a-half weeks. I was given the choice to wait until just over 40 weeks or take them out at closer to 38 weeks as my obstetrician was going away. I was assured that two weeks early was perfectly fine and actually for someone of my size to carry twins for that long was a fantastic achievement in itself.

The story my grandmother had told me of her twin pregnancy 50 years earlier was not easy to forget. Back then there were no ultrasounds and time spent in hospital after a baby was born could last weeks. Ma had not even known she was carrying twins. She went into hospital and gave birth to one baby and the nurses proceeded to care for her and the newborn. Congratulations and happiness erupted in the room. Several minutes later, Ma said she felt like there was still a baby inside and she wanted to push. The nurses thought they needed to calm her, saying, 'No, no, you have had your baby, everything is fine, don't worry.' But Ma really insisted she had to push! The doctor rushed back over and after a quick examination, said, 'Oh my goodness, you are having twins.' Then a second baby was born. It came as a total shock to everyone. Twins! A story you rarely hear of today with modern medicine.

So, on the 7th of February 2003 at 5.26 and 5.27 pm respectively, Zalie and Flynn were born at just under 38 weeks gestation. All of their fingers and toes were there and they looked perfect. We could not be happier. I was looking forward to five days in hospital to rest and recover before taking my babies home.

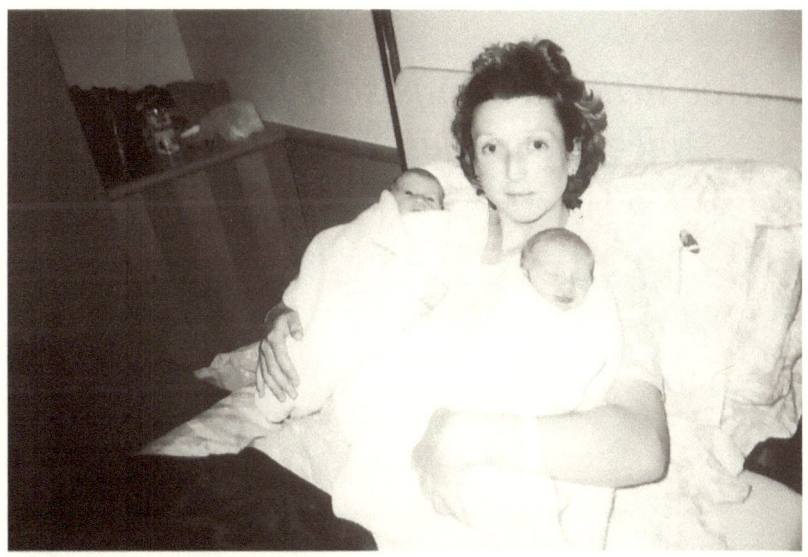

*Two little blessings sent from above;
twice the smiles, twice the love!*

CHAPTER 2

Didn't See It Coming

My beautiful girl and boy arrived home less than a week later to a very excited older brother and extended family looking forward to meeting them for longer than a quick hospital visit.

My rest in hospital was much needed and a large part of me had wanted to stay longer. Having the help of the nurses for all night feeds, while I was able to get some sleep, was wonderful. I was also recovering from major abdominal surgery, so finding the balance between caring for myself and being a mum to two newborns along with a two-year-old was starting to worry me. Could I not just stay in hospital a few more weeks? Oh, I know, not possible! But it sounded like the answer.

It had been suggested by both the nursing staff and my hospital paediatrician that the twins share the same cot after arriving home and for several weeks afterwards, as due to the closeness they had shared for the past nine months, they would settle better being together. I was also told that as they were born two weeks early, it would be more than likely they would sleep for 23 of the 24 hours a day, as in their eyes and according to their body clock, they were still not meant to be born. I thought this was quite bizarre, however it turned out to be right. I honestly thought I must be the best mother in the world for those first two weeks.

The twins slept all the time and I had to wake them day and night, every three to three-and-a-half hours, to feed them. This was not seeming so hard after all. Babies that had to be woken to be fed, left me with plenty of time to look after myself and to spend time with Bryce, who was like any typical two-year-old, wanting his Mum's attention. They were a blissful two weeks. I did have my husband at home on paternity leave so night feeds were not only my responsibility and my mum was visiting very regularly and enjoyed feeding the twins herself.

I had attempted breastfeeding in the beginning, whilst still in hospital, but could not produce enough milk to feed both babies, so they had ended up being completely bottle-fed by the time we left hospital. This was not a decision I made easily and, like many mums, I felt some guilt about this, but I had to do what I and my support team felt was best for the babies and myself. Not enough breast milk meant hungry babies. There were many discussions about this; my mum even said, 'Don't worry, you were a seventies baby placed straight onto the bottle and you turned out fine.' I don't know whether this was helpful or not, but, yes, I had turned out OK, so fair enough they would be fine with formula is what I then had to accept.

I think back now to the picture in my mind of two tiny babies laying side-by-side together, wrapped in their own blanket, content with each other's closeness and breathing and it still melts my heart. They were not big babies either: Zalie was born weighing 5 pounds 4 ounces and Flynn was 6 pounds 1 ounce. From very early on, we called Zalie a 'little bird', as she reminded us of a tiny fragile baby bird; she was just so small and fine.

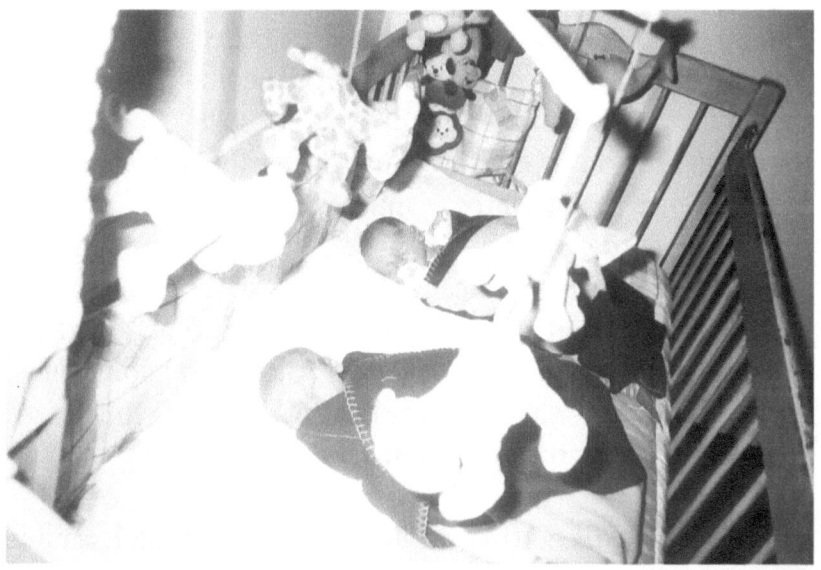

My thoughts that I must be the best mother in the world were somewhat short-lived, the two-week bliss of my babies sleeping 23 hours a day quickly moved onto two babies waking whenever they were hungry and wanting to be fed day and night. During those first few months, I don't think I ever fell apart completely, but I came close. I took on the advice from my maternal health nurse to try the feed-play-sleep routine for the twins. I found it worked and I really tried to stick to this from very early on. After a feed during the day, I would always make sure the twins stayed awake to play, even if they seemed tired. The play time would ensure I could settle them for sleep and they were tired enough to rest. It stopped the unnecessary waking for no reason and helped them both maintain a routine. They enjoyed 'Tummy Time', as we called it, laying on their back to play as young babies, then being rolled onto their tummy, raising their head to strengthen their neck muscles. We had interactive toys and mobiles to encourage their early progress.

The support my mother provided in that first year was wonderful. Literally every weekday for the first nine months she came round to our house to give me a rest, help to entertain Bryce, to stay on top of the constant bottle sterilising, the dirty nappies and washing. I managed to keep the house in some sort of order and Bryce was able to attend his swimming classes, gym and play dates with friends without having his mum constantly on edge or stressed trying to juggle, three children under three. I also looked forward to my mum's visits; it was nice to have the company of another adult while I was at home all day with three young children.

The twins enjoyed getting out for a daily walk in their double pram and we would take our dog.

I had even purchased a square skateboard attachment for the back of the double pram so that Bryce could enjoy coming along for our walks too, and when he got tired, he could just jump on the skateboard while I pushed. This was great for my fitness, clearing the head and getting out of the house. Timing it just after the twins feeding and play time would allow them to be tired and ideally fall asleep with the motion of the pram.

There is no denying I got tired and my head would hit the pillow hard at the end of each day. We always woke the twins for a feed around 11 pm, whether it had only been two-and-a-half or three hours since their last feed. When I say woke them, I mean they were picked up from their cot, still asleep, their nappies changed and given a bottle, burped and laid back down to continue sleeping, to encourage them to sleep through the night as best they could so that we could get a good stint of sleeping hours. A top-up is what my health nurse called it. More often than not, their eyes would not even open at this hour and they were happy to have a tummy top up before going back to sleep. It would only be on the odd occasion they would then wake at maybe 3 am, but more often it was 4 or 5 am as we worked towards an ideal six hours of overnight sleep. We hoped for a fairly similar feed timing routine for both of them in the early days. But we were always being respectful to the fact they were both so unique in their behaviours so we needed to be flexible as each day could be very different from the last.

Their first developmental milestones were also different. As they were brother and sister, did not look like twins and were not identical, I did not expect them to do things at the same time.

Zalie seemed to achieve her milestones before Flynn, sitting independently by eight months of age, progressing to crawling and then walking by 12 months. Whereas Flynn did not sit up by himself until 10 months of age and did not walk until nearly 14 months.

They were both very happy, healthy babies who enjoyed looking at your smiling face, interacting with family and friends. My regular maternal health nurse visits were at home in the early days, then we would go into their clinic. They were always positive. I was very proud of them, and at this stage, seemed to think I was holding it all together pretty well.

We managed our first family weekend away to a coastal town in Victoria, Inverloch, when the twins were about nine months old. Double pram packed, two of those crazy looking walkers where the babies sit and have a tray at the front of them to keep them occupied or allow them to eat while running their little legs underneath getting a workout. In some countries, these walkers are now actually banned due to safety reasons. The car was full of stuff, but the five of us enjoyed a break and the twins loved the experience of being somewhere else. I can still visualise them both as clear as day running in their walkers up and down the bitumen roads that wound through the coastal caravan park. Experiencing the sand in their toes on the beach was lovely to see.

As we approached the 12-month stage, it was time for another vaccine the MMR (measles, mumps and rubella) and I had discussions with my health nurse about this. Not that I am an anti-vaxxer, but it is really something I feel you should be comfortable to ask questions about and the fact that this vaccine was three shots in one did concern me. But, as the twins were both alert and healthy and they were starting to say their first words, there seemed to be no concerns or reasons why we would not go ahead with the government regulated vaccination programme. Bryce had been fine with it, so I booked Zalie and Flynn in. It had also been mentioned to me that with pre-school attendance or any childcare down the track, that the preference is for children to be up to date with their vaccinations for the safety of everyone.

We celebrated the twins' first birthday party with a large group of family and friends at a local park and playground which had lovely undercover seating. I made a long colourful caterpillar birthday cake. Zalie and Flynn thought it was wonderful. Zalie was taking steps and impressing everyone with her walking. Flynn, we had nicknamed 'Pooh Bear' as he was such a happy, cute bundle of smiles and very huggable. I honestly could not believe a year had passed since they were born.

At about six weeks of age, I had separated them from sleeping in the same cot and they both moved into their own bedrooms. Each room had its own cot, bookshelf with toybox attached and was decorated personally to suit their individual interests, which were really now starting to show as they moved into their second year.

Flynn was enjoying his Thomas the Tank Engine train and Zalie loved anything girly: Tinkerbell the fairy was a favourite.

They were starting to babble and sound out their first words – Dad, Dog, Mum, Nan – which was very exciting. Although their speech was not as strong as Bryce's at this age, they were trying.

As parents, it is only natural that we compare our children to each other, as this is often our best form of guidance. What one child does or when they hit a certain milestone, we then look at their siblings and expect this to be the same. For me, I often compared Zalie and Flynn's progress with that of Bryce's. Something that helped me to do this also were the photographs

I took, developed and placed in their individual photo albums. This was not the reason I kept such an extensive photo log, but I had wanted to give all of my children a lifetime of memories by keeping a photo album of them each from the day they were born. Rather than having to rummage through boxes of photos wondering which baby is which and how old they were, I kept a very detailed album.

Each of their albums has a photo at the front from when they were roughly nine months of age. Then, on the first page a tiny paint ink print of their foot on paper, which I did, this often took me several goes. At six weeks of age placing paint on your baby's tiny foot and getting a neat print on coloured cardboard, could be tricky. Then the albums began with a couple of ultrasound photos, hospital photos with family who visited just after they were born, their first bath, in hospital and various cute shots. Then, as we went home, I kept taking photos, a couple a week in the early days ('three weeks and one day – enjoying a hug with Nan'), ('six weeks and five days – first walk with mum in chest harness'). I marked monthly milestones with a photo and kept a record with photos, comments and fun stickers, weekly until a year old. Then after they turned one, it was just a couple a month, usual photos for special outings, the zoo, birthday parties, holidays, right up until the age of four years.

On the inside back cover, I even made note of the first time they did things or achieved a milestone. First hiccup, laugh, first time they rolled over, talked, crawled, walked.

I also noted for my babies the cost of a carton of milk, newspaper, cinema ticket, things like that, who the prime minister was at the time. It was time consuming, but so enjoyable and such a joy for my children and myself to look back at; something I can pass onto them to show their own children one day.

As I said, these albums helped me as they meant I could look back at photos and they would trigger memories, and I really enjoyed keeping these photo logs, it gave me something to focus on and to be a bit arty, enjoy something creative for myself, while trying to be some kind of super mum.

Both the twins had spoken their first word at around seven months of age: 'Dad', 'Mum', 'dog'. The 'd' of 'Dad', the 'm' of 'Mum' and 'd' of 'dog', just as my older son had done. I had noted this in the back of their individual photo albums. Which was really helpful, because as a mum if we don't write things down, we often forget!

So, as they moved towards 15-18 months of age, I was expecting them to be more talkative than what they were, more than just the occasional word, as Bryce was fully conversational with sentences at 18 months of age. However, I understand that we are all different and reach our milestones when we are ready.

As my grandmother had twins, I would often chat with her about how she coped, how her babies developed and what difficulties she had being a mother of two the same age. I remember distinctly Ma would always say to me, Joanne don't worry my twin boys did not talk until age four. So with me being concerned that I was not getting more conversation from my one-and-a-half-year-olds, it should not have been a worry. However we try and be as optimistic and relaxed as parents –that's natural – but it is also natural to compare, not just within your own family but within your social networks.

The twins enjoyed going to play groups with me and their older brother, they enjoyed going to gymbaroo, jumping on the trampoline at home and swimming at the local pool. They loved watching TV, they both had favourite ABC Kids programmes. Flynn adored *Thomas the Tank Engine*. Zalie loved anything that involved fairies, *Peppa Pig*, girly stuff. They enjoyed going to the library, looking through books at home and every night story time before bed, was loved.

Zalie and Flynn were both great eaters from an early age; as babies you could puree or mash pretty much every vegetable combination and they would devour it, and they could not pass up a bowl of ice-cream after dinner a couple of times a week. Zalie also loved her meat, whereas Flynn was more a raw vegetables man. They were smiley, happy kids – there was no denying that.

But it was not just the lack of words; I was also noticing that Zalie seemed a bit more distant than she used to be. I would often call out her name, but she would not turn around or acknowledge that I was talking to her. My first thought was that she was playing a game with me. She was typically smiley and cheeky, a mass of curly brown hair that was so easy to style, and she loved being tickled and playing hide and seek. However, I was starting to see my little girl a bit more in her own world, rather than in ours. When on the change table, she would look around and to the sides rather than look at me. Her eye contact had changed. She would stand by the window and look out, as you do, into the garden or when people were arriving at the front door, but instead of waving or trying to say hello, she would be chewing with her teeth on the wooden windowsill, like a little rabbit gnaws on a carrot. This did not seem right! I would tell her 'no', but it didn't help.

Didn't See It Coming

I tried putting taste deterrents on the timber, but that didn't work. Every front windowsill of the house had teeth marks along it, and not just a few either. She would also put things into her mouth that you really should not: sand, playdough, tanbark and on such a regular basis that it seemed like she was craving something in them that was not in her diet. These things started to worry me.

Three months after I gave birth to the twins, my hair started to fall out and I went into a panic. Imagine standing in the shower, rinsing out the shampoo and conditioner, with clumps of hair falling into your hands. It was predominantly on my left side. I went to see my local doctor, who told me it was stress. Not that I was feeling stressed at the time, but apparently it takes three months after a stressful situation for your body to really show the signs of how traumatic something was. In other words, three months after I had given birth to my twins, my body was saying, 'Ha, gosh, that was hard on me, that took a lot out, so let's just shed some hair.' I really could not believe it and did some investigating myself into medical trauma, spoke to a few people and it was confirmed that, yes, this was such a thing.

I covered it up with hair bands and got on with life. What could I do? My hair grew back, although never to quite the same thickness, but I shook it off and moved on.

I mention it now because three months after the twins had their MMR vaccine, I started to notice something different about them. Weird! I don't know, but they had been typically developing until around the 15-month mark. This was when I first started to notice changes. Was the stress of that vaccine something they were now showing to me? Three vaccines in one.

Zalie and Flynn, age - 18 months

*Mother of twins,
classic overachiever.*

CHAPTER 3

Pardon?

It was not just me being an over-concerned mum. My own mother had mentioned to me a few things she had noticed about Zalie's interaction with her and my father that didn't seem right. The twins both attended a small local playgroup along with Bryce, and Zalie's play habits in particular were different. She did not interact with the other children, preferring to play on her own with playdough, often putting it into her mouth, or she played with balls, collecting and throwing them. Her social interaction seemed to be delayed. Flynn was more social, and his eye contact was fine, but he had a very strong interest in trains and really only wanted to play with them.

Another issue we were having was getting the twins, particularly Zalie, to stay in her bed at night after putting her to sleep. The warm bath, warm drink, bedtime story routine, we were letting her body unwind and relax, and she was obviously tired. But would not fall asleep, she would climb out of her cot over and over again. Just straight over the side and come out of her room. It became such a problem, we had to place a lock on her door from the outside and we would lock her in her room. We often found her two hours later out of her cot, and fast asleep, spread-eagle in the middle of her bedroom floor where she would then be carefully lifted into her cot. This same issue had also become a problem for Flynn, whether he was copying his sister or doing it for his own reasons, as we also had to place a lock on the outside of his bedroom door.

Going to this extreme, which I thought it was at the time, placing an external lock on bedroom doors seemed barbaric. But it was coming to a point of safety and sanity – safety for the twins, to encourage them to no longer climb over the sides of their cots if the door was locked and we even removed all toys from their bedroom floor so there was absolutely no incentive to leave the cot when they were obviously tired – sanity for the rest of the family. There are only so many times at the end of a long day, you feel like putting a child back into their bed for the fifth time. It was like they were over-wired energiser bunnies when they should have been sleeping.

My health nurse suggested I reconnect with the paediatrician I had not seen for a few months and discuss my, and now her, concerns.

Pardon?

No one likes to be worried about their children's development, but modern life dictates that certain milestones should happen at this time or in this way, and as soon as they don't, we start to worry. Our materialistic world, in which we have access to information at the touch of a phone or iPad, sometimes tells us too much too quickly. Sixteen years ago now, when my twins were age two, I did not walk around with an iPhone constantly in my hand or within arm's reach. I went downstairs at night into our little study nook at the back of the rumpus room, really the size of a storage cupboard where our desktop computer was located and started to look up information regarding toddlers and their development. I went to the library to look for books regarding pre-school development.

Researching poor eye contact, repetitive play and putting weird things in your mouth, the word 'autism' kept popping up. Pardon? I had never heard of the word before, nor really known what it meant.

What was autism? Furthermore, how could a little girl who had all her working limbs, was not of poor sight, could hear, had started to talk a few words and was very pretty have anything wrong with her? No, this did not sound correct. It couldn't be right. What does a social disability even mean?

It was not long after I came across the word 'autism', while scouring for information one night that our then paediatrician mentioned to me his concerns, and the word 'autism' was raised again. He felt that the characteristics that Zalie was showing through her social interaction, play habits and avoiding eye contact were strong signs of someone with this condition. Furthermore, he also raised concerns to me regarding Flynn, although Flynn's eye contact was good, his preference for solo play and with the same toys and the way he lined them up was also consistent with autistic traits.

Well, what do you say to that? As a parent, it hits you like a blow to the stomach. Why was this happening? What had I done wrong? How did this happen? I knew little, basically nothing, of what this meant and what our future direction would be.

He suggested to me that his thoughts and opinion would be stage one; that from here on, I would need to take both the twins to a child psychiatrist for formal testing and diagnosis and if his thoughts were correct. If confirmed by the psychiatrist, I would then be referred to the Austin Hospital for further testing and guidance.

In the interim, I was told, I should look at some 'early intervention' and was recommended to take them both to a speech therapist, and was given the name of a lady called Kerrie, who had experience working with children delayed in their speech for various reasons, including possible autism. It was also suggested I go home and do some reading and was handed a whole pile of paperwork and names of people to call for support. Naturally, the next step for me was to burst into tears. I am an emotional person, whether receiving good or bad news, when it comes to my children, and with those emotions come tears. In this case, a lot of tears.

It is really not something you run home and ring all your friends and family about to share the news. In my eyes at that stage, this was not good news that I wanted to share with anyone. Those who knew I had an appointment contacted me, such as my mum. But otherwise, I kept it to myself for a while, until I could get my head around what the next step would be, and who I would first reach out to for information, guidance and assistance. When your world is suddenly turned upside down overnight, you shut down, you don't want to talk to anyone and you need time to process and reassess. I think I walked around in a daze for a week afterwards.

Putting my emotions aside and trying to move forward, practically for Zalie and Flynn, what I soon learned was nothing happens quickly, in this world of assessment and diagnosis. It was not as if the next week or month I could walk into a psychiatrist with my letter of referral and my two two-year-olds. This was going to be a long process.

I had been working casually and placing both Zalie and Flynn in childcare one day per week for social interaction and to learn a routine, other than ours at home, whilst Bryce was at four-year-old kindergarten (we also call it kinder or pre-school, so you will see all three terms used throughout this book). They enjoyed this day at day-care but were tired and drained by the end of it, and with both of them preferring to play independently, looking forward, this time at day care was not really giving them any great benefits, it just gave me a break.

They were, however, enjoying swimming lessons one morning a week. We had found a great local swim centre that allowed children from the age of two to be in the water without a parent. I had previously put one on each of my arms and swam around with them or put them in float rings.

These individual lessons were lovely. The twins loved the sensory feel of the water ('sensory', a word that would come into our lives often over the next 15 years) and I had a break and so enjoyed watching them learn a lifesaving skill of water safety and to be having fun while doing it. It was 30 minutes of bliss.

I can't say the 20 minutes afterwards in the change room were exactly bliss, chasing around two-year-olds wanting a quick warm shower and dressing them, but you have to take the good with the bad.

I had gone through so many emotions; I could now truly see things were not as they should be with the twins' development, and I was looking for someone or something to blame – a reason for why this had happened.

Australia did not seem to have a lot of information at that stage; many of my resources were coming from America. From what I could gather, they seemed to have a lot more answers to questions I had. As they have such a large population, they seemed to have more experience and examples to learn from.

I was questioning what may have gone wrong with my pregnancy, whether it was something I had done or eaten. Was it something I had fed the twins when there were young? Was it because I did not breastfeed and, as such, denied them nutrients? Was it the trauma on their small bodies and brain from the MMR vaccine? I was finding a lot of talk about that in my research. Was it hereditary? Did I let them watch too much TV when they were babies? Should I have played them Beethoven and read more books? These were just some of the guilt questions I was asking myself.

Pardon?

Firstly, I delved into the MMR vaccine scenario, and it turned out there were many conversations being had in the late 1990s or early 2000s regarding the health risks of having the vaccine and people who blamed this triple antigen for changes in their children's development, including links to autism. This, I knew, would take years to prove or disprove. Also, if Bryce, my eldest, had the vaccine and he was fine, why would this have been different with the twins? Unless their brain genetics were such that the autism was already there and just needed a trigger.

My research also found a common point of discussion that we all have a thread of autism in us; it is just to what degree. There was talk that it can run in families, that it was hereditary. It was a 1:5 ratio. Which meant of five people with autism, four would be boys and only one was a girl. My husband had a niece with autism and an older brother who may have been on the spectrum – could this be related to what was going on with my twins?

There was actually quite a bit of information out there, it seemed, if you were prepared to look hard. Not all of it was helpful – some was just confusing and disheartening.

But there were also positive stories, famous people in our history, who had lived full rewarding lives who had autism: Hans Christian Andersen, Albert Einstein, Andy Warhol.

Even so, I felt quite alone. I had the family to talk to about this, but I knew I had to be the one to work through all my worries and concerns and find a pathway forward.

Even speaking to my grandmother, who was an avid reader, she knew little or nothing of the word 'autism' and really wanted me to explain it to her. But at this stage, I did not know how, and I did not know enough to even explain it to myself!

However, I don't do slow; I am not a waiter but a doer. The pathway apparently for now I was told for the twins, was not to sit around and wait for further confirmation from specialists, but to access early intervention as soon as possible. I was not clear exactly what this meant, but I had been given a few phone numbers of places within our local area and surrounds who could help me further on this pathway.

Reaching out to our first speech therapist was a lot of help and finding someone who knew where to start with my twins' speech inability. We were given basic play activities that would initiate the prompting to say words or attempt to say words. Games that required Zalie and Flynn to use their mouth muscles and strengthen them for speech, like simply blowing bubbles, and Kerrie helped fill in some gaps for me regarding her experience of two-year-olds with lack of speech.

It would be early intervention and guidance from experienced people that gave me a ray of sunshine when I felt like crawling into a very dark cave. I had made a few phone calls one Thursday morning, explaining my situation with the twins and this new path I would be travelling down, which I really needed support with. There was one place that had a waiting list. When I made another call, they said, 'Maybe we can help you next school term, can you call back?', but it was my third phone call to a place called EPIC (now Noah's Ark), based at RMIT in Bundoora, which gave the most hope. I was put through to someone immediately who made an appointment with me for the following Tuesday. They said come along, we can have a chat, meet Zalie and Flynn and you can see the

Pardon?

support we offer and sit in on one of our early intervention classes. This was great news.

In those early months of the interim diagnosis I was so determined, having done a lot of reading and investigating, that I could fix this. Something I look back on now, after many years and ask, fix what? They were never broken... What was I thinking? You can't fix autism; you have to work with it. Autism does not go away. It is part of the person, you can make it positive or negative, love them for who they are and what they can give, their uniqueness. But back then, when I was thrown into a whole different world and way of thinking, that was not something I understood or appreciated.

Zalie and Flynn, age - 2 years and 10 mths

I am different, not less.

– Dr Temple Grandin

CHAPTER 4

Climbing A Mountain

Early intervention came to us in leaps and bounds; it was like a hand reached down from heaven to guide us along. They were called EPIC (Education Programme for Infants and Children) and were linked to RMIT.

We were assigned a wonderful lady by the name of Chris who came to our home and met us at the support centre on the university grounds. I explained to her we were awaiting an appointment with a children's psychiatrist to be given possibly an autism diagnosis for Zalie and also Flynn.

She was introduced to my twins and immediately wanted to help us. She had a wealth of experience and fully understood the journey we as a family were about to take. She said, 'Joanne, you have done the right thing, the process of formal diagnosis is a long one, but while you wait you must act.'

Here come the happy tears – I had found a kind, caring person who understood and could help. I did not feel alone anymore. We would be introduced to other families in the same situation. I would meet other mothers, feeling overwhelmed like me, and we could have a coffee and a chat.

The twins would be placed in a small group, like a playgroup, which educates and teaches. They would attend this group once a week, I would also be there to learn how to help them, and each family group would have a trained autism specialist with them whilst attending this class to guide appropriate behaviours and learning of social and communication skills.

Chris had worked with many pre-school-aged children with autism. Any question I needed to ask she had an answer for. In her eyes, Zalie and Flynn both had developmental delays and whatever the outcome was formally, they needed support now to help them be ready for pre-school and beyond. Chris acknowledged the lack of eye contact from Zalie, her obvious sensory issues. Flynn's strong interest in only certain things and both of their preferences to play not together or with other children, but rather next to, whilst staying very much in their own world.

Autism, I was told, was a social disability.

Sensory issues for Zalie meant certain foods she was not comfortable to eat or taste; often she would remove her clothing for no reason, other than it felt more comfortable to have it not touching her skin. Sudden loud noises she did not enjoy, or the constant buzz of a busy room, she would step back and retreat, either to a chair on her own or another room altogether.

I soon learnt that Zalie's sensory system was heightened. What a noise sounded like to us, a taste in the mouth or something on her skin could be amplified for her 10 times. She really enjoyed the feeling of spinning around and the visual of fluttering her fingers in front of her eyes.

On the other hand, Flynn's sensory system was really only bothered by noise, something sudden and loud, really, really upset him or, like Zalie, the busyness of a crowded room, shopping centres were not his thing.

We would receive home support and, 'Your twins need a communication system that works for them,' I was told. 'They are not speaking but need to be able to be understood, to feel like they can interact with you by communicating other than with words.' They would both grab my hand and walk me to what they needed or get it themselves, but they would not point and could not verbalise their needs. This confused me at first, until I was shown the Picture Exchange Communication System (PECS).

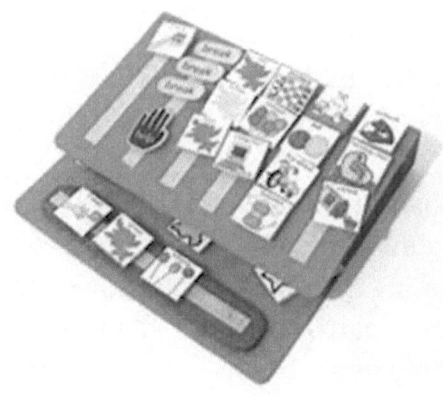

PECS was presented to us as an A5 hard cover folder that contained small, laminated pictures of everyday things, food, toys, drink, animals, numbers, with a Velcro strip at the base of the front cover. The twins were to place on the Velcro strip the words 'I want' which was on a laminated card and a picture of the item – be it food, drink or a toy, for example – and hand the strip to me to communicate what they wanted. Their eyesight was fine, they could see what the pictures meant. It was a matter of understanding this process and realising if they did it correctly, they could get what they needed at the time.

When at home, both Zalie and Flynn's communication folders would be placed in a central part of the house, usually the kitchen for easy access, and they would go to it when they wanted something from me – food, toys, to go outside, to go out in the car, many different things. They would construct a small sentence and hand the strip to me or another adult who was available, to communicate their wants. With the next step being attempting to say the constructed sentence, that was the aim. The small folders had a handle on the side that meant the twins could carry their communication system with them wherever they went. If we were heading off to visit their grandparents' house, they would pick up their folders or if we were going to swimming lessons, or playgroup. They now had something to encourage their words a way to communicate that did not involve grabbing someone by the hand and leading them to their need or trying to access it themselves.

Chris would visit our home once a week, sometimes twice if I was having an issue with something, and work with the twins – reinforcing their communication system, adding new laminated picture cards to their folders when they wanted to access something new.

It was the winter of 2005 when the twins attended their first session in the early intervention programme which was like a play group. We had been in contact with EPIC for about a month and were starting to understand how to use the PECS. They were just over two-and-a-half years old by that stage. We were still seeing our speech therapist Kerrie and attempting to use the picture exchange system with her also.

It was lovely for me to finally meet some other parents and have a support network. Most of them also had other children like we did, and were families trying to juggle life, plus the requirements of this new reality – our new normal.

It became obvious not long after we started with EPIC, that Flynn would grasp most things quicker than Zalie, as his autistic traits were not as strong.

Our appointment with the child psychiatrist finally came around just as the twins were turning three years of age in February 2006. This was the second step of three on our pathway to an autism diagnosis. There would be two appointments each and a report written for both Zalie and Flynn. It was noted that Flynn presented as an appealing little boy with fair hair. He walked in with his Thomas the Tank Engine train toy and his play, voice skills and interactions were observed intently and discussed. I was asked numerous questions and a documented history was taken from his birth to the present moment. He was very pleased that I had been proactive following our initial meeting with their paediatrician many months ago and had a pathway moving forward for Flynn. That the plan and my hope would be for him to attend three-year-old pre-school that year and to keep attending his weekly early intervention sessions at EPIC and his speech classes.

Flynn spoke some single words at that meeting, but his language development was noted as being delayed. He would babble in a sing song voice to himself and put a lot of toys to his mouth. His eye contact was noted as good, but his play was isolated and repetitive. He could tolerate everyday noises, such as a vacuum cleaner, but any unusual noise in close proximity or out of the ordinary really affected him. His hearing test at age two years was good, even though he had a history of glue ear at approximately 18 months of age. The report was actually five pages long and very in-depth.

He was given a Childhood Autism Rating Scale (CARS) score of 31.5, just above the threshold for an autism diagnosis.

The CARS scores ranged from 15 to 60. Which I later learnt, a score below 30 meant individuals were in the non-autistic range, while scores between 30 and 36.5 indicated mild to moderate autism, and scores from 37 to 60 indicated severe autism. This CARS score would be needed for me to access support and funding for Zalie and Flynn and for the educational systems and governments in our country to recognise this now and in their future.

Zalie was noted as an appealing little girl with fair hair and blue eyes. Her eye contact was poor and she would frequently put a variety of toys in her mouth. She did not show any imaginative play, the day was quite warm and although she was dressed appropriately, she tried to remove her clothes, even when repeatedly told not to. At times, she gazed across the room and seemed to be in her own little world. No recognisable words were heard from Zalie. She eventually removed all her clothes and was quite upset at the end of the session.

I told the psychiatrist the plan for Zalie moving forward in that year was the same as Flynn, to hopefully attend three-year-old kindergarten with weekly visits to EPIC for early intervention.

Zalie received a CARS score of 41 which was comfortably above the threshold for a diagnosis of autism.

Zalie and Flynn were both then given an official provisional diagnosis of autism, in addition to a language/communication disorder for Flynn and a significant language communication disorder for Zalie. Wow! We would be keeping our speech therapist.

So, with my beautiful twins now looking at being labelled, at this stage, with the word 'autism', our next step on this road was an appointment at Austin Health where two clinical psychologists and a speech pathologist would meet with us and assess the twins and give the final diagnosis.

By this stage they were both three years old and I was well aware this was going to happen – it was just all the official terminology and ratings, which I was being told now. It really at that point did not change anything, we were already travelling this road, doing our best to access services we needed.

The final required appointment at the Austin Hospital with speech pathologists and their psychology department and the eventual report that confirmed all of the above did not arrive in my lap until June 2007, by which stage the twins were four years and three months old.

My goodness, what a long process that was. A three-step process that took over two years.

If I had waited that long before I started early intervention with Zalie and Flynn, waited for all the formalities, we would have been two years behind in progress. This taught me very early on the only way forward was to always be pro-active, think of the next thing you can do to support your children and be planning it. Talk to people, ask questions, look for support.

What did shake me most with all this was that Zalie was given a CARS score of 41, which meant that, in the eyes of many, she had severe autism. Now severe is a strong word. The storm coming your way, is not mild or moderate, it's severe! This did flatten me for a while, I knew she had some challenges, and goodness she was doing some bizarre things at times. But was she really severe? What was the outcome for her future possibilities, with the word severe attached to every document and paperwork that went with her name for the years to come.

I knew then I did not like this numbering system, this CARS score. It was often even mentioned in conversation with people I associated with in the autism world.

'What was your CARS score?' people would ask. In other words, what number was hanging over your child's head.

This number was never changed, she was never reassessed and given a higher or lower number still to this day, that is what her CARS score is, regardless of her achievements or how far she has come.

But it is just a number, an assessment tool used in the medical world and it became irrelevant to me as we moved forward. It took me a long while to realise this, the number and the word severe played on my mind, but on the other hand gave me determination.

I never wanted anyone to call my beautiful little girl severe. Her autism would not be severe, it would not be how she would be known.

I soon learnt not to let the medical world dictate the capacity of your child, as so much is up to you and the support you give and surround them with.

They no longer give a CARS score, I believe, and thank goodness for that, because in my eyes it did not really help. You get funding and assistance because your child has a diagnosis of autism, and you don't receive more or less support because you have a higher number, but that higher number is hard to deal with from a parent's perspective. It can make you feel like things are possibly out of reach, which they should not be.

Autism where the little things are never little, and every milestone is a celebration.

CHAPTER 5

Trying To Blend In

As we opened the doors wider and stepped out further into the world, the twins began three-year-old kinder the same year as Bryce started primary school. It was fortunate for our family that the pre-school in walking distance from our home, which Bryce had attended before them, was very nurturing and inclusive. It was run by a lovely teacher called Kim who welcomed the twins with open arms and fully engaged them in the programme, whilst also taking on board their PECS communication system and their individual behaviours.

I recall that first day, the proud tears watching your firstborn head off to school, and also my twins stepping out on their own away from me, under the care of other adults. But also under the eye of other parents, who would notice very quickly that Zalie in particular had a different way of looking at the world.

In the months prior, particularly over the Christmas holidays before the twins started pre-school, I had gone down the road of trying to toilet train them both. Ideally, it was the preference/pre-requisite that your son or daughter be toilet trained before starting three-year-old kinder.

It had been of great concern to me, how we would tackle toilet training, particularly doing two at once. It was the PECS system that came to our rescue, and with the help of Chris from EPIC, we put together a visual strip that showed the steps in pictures of what was required for the twins to do in order to become independent on the toilet. The Christmas holidays was the perfect time, we were home relaxed, the twins could wear little to no clothing and I could keep a close watch on them, make sure they drank plenty of water and reminded them what to do.

Flynn took to this like a duck to water. As with anything, you are teaching your children to feel like they have done the right thing, that you are proud of them and you reward them as an acknowledgement of their achievements, so each time the twins used their communication strip or the visuals we had on the wall representing the same process, their reward for making it to the toilet was food – they both loved Pringles chips – so that's how it worked. Make it to the toilet, no accidents, then you get a small handful of chips. It was not always food, sometimes Flynn would request his Thomas the Tank Engine train (he had a fancy gold Thomas that was his favourite). But he must have just been ready. As I was astounded and so proud to tell everyone that after just two weeks he was toilet trained. I could not believe it, and honestly just looked at him with amazement. 'Flynny,' as we called him, 'you are just wonderful, you don't need nappies anymore, you are a big boy now'.

Some children who do not struggle with communication have trouble grasping this, and here you after two weeks. Amazing!

From then on, I never doubted his ability to understand, no matter what the circumstances if you explained and demonstrated in a way that worked for him: he could do anything.

For Zalie, it took a while longer. I think she kind of understood the process and certainly loved the reward of pringles chips. (Potato crisps have always been one of her favourite things to this day, I learnt early on that the crunch of the chip and the taste of the salt, were something her food sensory system just loved).

However, other things were more interesting, and in her mind if she did not make it to the toilet, oh well, mum would clean up after her. I was patient, and I think as Flynn had only taken two weeks, it did not help her cause. But after two months of trying with not much progress, I was becoming a little cranky. So, one warm Saturday when it was just her and I at home, I made her drink a lot of water. I was not going to be happy to accept an accident, so I followed her around, showing her the picture strip, asking if she needed to go. I finally thought that she must be close to bursting, so I took her to the bathroom, sat her down on the kiddy toilet seat and waited, the whole time holding in my hands a container of Pringles and tub of bubbles with a wand to blow them

– her two most favourite things in the whole world. She was saying 'chip, chip', but I would not let her move. She sat on that toilet for half an hour – nothing – and by then she had also started to cry, yet still nothing. It was about then the front doorbell rang, and I was in a spot, do I answer it and risk her jumping off the toilet and all our hard work and tears would be wasted or do I leave the person standing there. Fortunately, it was a friend dropping by and I yelled out to them to go around the back. They could hear Zalie's loud crying and carry on and must have thought the worst of me. Zalie had now been sitting there for 45 minutes. They let themselves in the back door, and it was just at that time that Zalie finally gave in – *tinkle tinkle tinkle*. It was working! I clapped my hands, danced and smiled till she giggled, and I gave her the biggest hug. Yes, that was what I wanted you to do, it was like 'bing' the light came on. I handed her the whole tube of Pringles chips and we went outside to meet our friend and blew bubbles to celebrate.

From then on, she got it. *Tinkle, tinkle* and she got Pringles and bubbles.

So much was her want for both of these, she rarely had an accident again.

Trying To Blend In

Flynn adored pre-school and trying to learn how to interact with teachers and peers. He was very angelic in his appearance and his nature. Naturally a very kind boy, we found other children were somewhat drawn to him. There were always children who wanted to play with Flynn even though his play skills were not that interactive. So often he would play and others would play next to him. At such a young age, three-year-olds are all still finding their way, so Flynn blended in nicely.

Kim, his teacher, would tell me how much Flynn loved the slide; he would go up and down over and over again. Then take his favourite trucks and run them down the slide. Playing on the slide would also involve other children, so Flynn could interact without having to talk that much.

This was positive to see. Not all play situations involve communication. Just knowing someone is near you or playing next to you can help to start form friendships. In those early years, Flynn did receive party invitations and was asked to play at friends' houses sometimes.

With the support from the pre-school staff, I had introduced Flynn and Zalie to the pre-school parents with a small amount of information so there would be understanding. This was done with just a typed note given to everyone.

Not that you want to scare people away, but just so they understand. This was welcomed by parents, who would then ask questions, take the time to chat and even share positive experiences or interactions that their child may have had with the twins, while at pre-school. I found this a relief, because as a mum of children with additional needs, we do often feel one step behind everyone else, worried what others think – we should not be, but that is easier said than done, particularly in the early years when you are hoping for your children to form friendships.

Zalie took to pre-school a little differently than Flynn. Her interaction with the teacher, Kim, was greater and she needed the adult support. She would be the one sitting on the teacher's lap at story time, while the other children sat cross legged in front of the teacher. Kim use to laugh as Zalie would come and lay on her lap and get her back rubbed every time she wanted to pass wind. The upside of this was that Zalie would often then model this behaviour for other children, sitting in the teacher's chair while holding a book up and pretending she was reading to the class.

Zalie would rarely interact directly with the other children but would instead sit at a table next to them and play with playdough or draw. She would put a lot of things in her mouth, so staff did have to keep an eye on her. This was due to her heightened sensory system and the need to taste. Playdough was a favourite, followed closely by tan bark and sand when she was outside, which she really enjoyed the crunch of, but it was terribly unhygienic and not good for her. To deal with this issue of her liking for non-edible food items. I would send Zalie to pre-school with what I called a 'crunchy foods grazing box'. In it, I would place foods such as raw pasta, crackers, hundreds and thousands. She would eat these and have access to them before outside play time. It gave her the sensory crunch she was craving and encouraged her to eat the food rather than the tan bark and sand.

Interestingly, we noticed early on that she had a strong eye for fine detail and if there was the smallest speck on the dark carpet, whether it was a sequin or a bit of fluff, maybe glitter, she would pick it up, examine it, maybe take it and hand it to Kim. Kim would then ask if she wished to keep it or put it in the bin.

It seemed what other children did not really notice, her eyes would gravitate towards.

An eye for detail would turn out to be such a fortunate and valuable quality for an artist, which I was not aware Zalie was at her young age.

Three-year-old kinder sessions were manageable for the twins with two-and-a-half-hour sessions on a Monday morning and Friday afternoon. However, the following year when they progressed to four-year-old pre-school, it did become much harder for them.

Zalie was entitled to an aide at four-year-old pre-school, which was brought to my attention both by Chris at EPIC and Kim the kinder teacher. Although Flynn would also benefit from additional support, his needs were not strong enough to gain him funding for an aide. Zalie received funding to cover an aide for eight hours. She would attend pre-school for two six-hour sessions a week, with an aide for four hours of each day. The twins both found six-hour sessions very long and tiring. They were the only pre-schoolers who both had their own little sleep tent down on the carpet. With a special blanket inside. If the day felt too long or their sensory system was overloaded, with the busyness of 26 children in a room. Both Zalie and Flynn could retreat to their tent for some downtime, whether that was a nap or just to chill out. It was really lovely to see this acceptance from both the teachers and students. Kids would often ask, 'Where is Flynn?' Another would answer, 'In his tent.' That was all OK as he was not judged any differently, and sometimes a friend would even pop their head in and say hello, maybe stay for a visit.

The times it did get tough for me as a mum were when there was a special day at kinder, such as a parents' morning tea or the like, when all mums or dads would come along and stay for a while, participate in a programme, and enjoy the company of their children at kinder.

Zalie and Flynn were usually happy if I ever visited during their day; it was exciting for them. But the downside, which is not uncommon for children on the autism spectrum, is the feeling of being overwhelmed, that there is too much going on, too much noise, things would be out of routine and they would start to feel uncomfortable, which would lead to behaviours that are considered by others to be alarming or unacceptable. In the twins' eyes, Mum had her place at home looking after us and at kinder we had the teachers. When these two worlds over-lapped, as much as they wanted them to, these occasions did not always go well. Emotions and sensory issues were heightened. This meant, more often than not, I learnt to sense when things were about to turn pear-shaped and would make a quick exit. Maybe only enjoying half of the scheduled afternoon visit or retreating outside for a break. Without trying to raise too much attention. I always had to be adaptable and pre-empt what may happen if we don't make a quick move now, we could be dealing with a meltdown in the next few minutes, so let's just go. Sometimes, I would have an excuse already prepared, such as an appointment or similar that we had to leave for. Other times I was just honest and said simply, 'Our time's up. Flynn or Zalie, or both, are finding it all a bit much now, we need to go home.' Other parents were usually understanding, even if it was a birthday party or social gathering. At such a young age, the twins were never bothered by this, but often I was, wondering what others were thinking. Didn't I know how to control my own children? Did I not discipline them enough at home? These were just a couple of thoughts that would go through my mind. I did learn in later years to develop a thicker skin and not worry nearly as much. It takes a while to understand autism, and how suddenly you find it difficult to cope socially, feeling overwhelmed and not in control of your own emotions.

Pre-school (or kinder) is the first time your child is cared for by others in an education setting. They learn a lot, but they are also somewhat wrapped in cotton wool as they are constantly nurtured and cared for. It is like one big family. They are a special couple of years. Often, it's the kinder photographs you look back at as some of the more memorable ones taken. They are always cute.

Pre-school sets you up for school and they advise you on whether your child is ready or not to move to the next stage, to start school, as a Prep. This was a trickier situation for Zalie and Flynn, it was not just a simple decision of ready for school or not, their education setting would need to be quite specific and able to support their needs at that time. As they would both be turning five at the beginning of the year they would start school, there was no rush to send them on if they were not ready. However, repeating four-year-old kinder was not really an option. I found this quite a stressful time – what to do? They both needed a smaller educational setting. They were not ready for a mainstream prep programme, with twenty five-year-olds all demanding the attention of one teacher. Would they ever be ready, was my other worry. They were both still having a lot of speech and language issues at this stage, only four years old. Zalie struggled to put more than two words together. Flynn could manage a small sentence. The PECS communication system was still proving to be very helpful.

After much deliberation with the pre-school teacher, Kim, Chris from EPIC and myself visiting various post pre-school options for children on the autism spectrum. I had decided the twins would be enrolled at the same school but in two different education settings. Flynn would be placed in a pre-prep programme based at Montmorency Primary School, a small school with only 110 students. There would be five to six students in the class with a teacher and aide support. They would mix with the mainstream students at lunch and recess but be taught in a smaller classroom. The class would be all boys, not for any particular reason other than that was who had enrolled.

This programme was actually run by Diamond Valley Special Developmental School (DVSDS), who have a large campus, for children with additional needs, aged from 5-18 years. However, for those students who were close to being able to be schooled in a mainstream setting and could interact with minimal assistance but needed extra support with education and communication, they offered what they called Base or Satellite Rooms. For parents, it also gave the sense and hope of support and future progress. The students were part of a local primary school but taught in a smaller more personal setting. The plan was that the following year Flynn could progress to the primary school Bryce was at as a mainstream prep student, he would turn six years old at the start of his prep year if this was his pathway. I was so excited that Flynn was being accepted into the base room at age five. Pre-prep programmes were very hard to find, but we had one in our local community. What was also so helpful is that a bus would come to the front of our house each morning and collect Flynn and drop him to school, then also bring him home in the afternoon.

Zalie needed a lot more support than Flynn at this stage. She would be based at Diamond Valley Special Developmental School for one year, with the hope that with some intense work and focus on her behaviours and communication she could progress to a Base Room at a local primary school the following year. Her class would also have six students in it, with a teacher and an aide. Being based at DVSDS would also give Zalie the opportunity to join in the horse-riding programme they ran at the school. Each week on a Wednesday she would get the opportunity to learn to interact with and ride a horse on the school grounds, which would be wonderful. Animal therapy, I would learn as we travelled this road, would be so beneficial.

With the twins reaching school age the last day at kinder was very emotional saying good-bye to the teacher and assistants. They participated with the other pre-schoolers in a graduation ceremony, including black gown and cap. It was gorgeous. This also meant that our time with EPIC, the early intervention programme, and the wonderful support from Chris, would be coming to an end.

For three years, Chris and the EPIC staff had helped us to navigate through so many challenges in those early years. Speech, finding alternative ways to communicate, tackling behaviour issues, toilet training, settling into pre-school and now the progression into the school environment.

They helped me to organise funding for the twins' future education. Children with additional needs are entitled to apply for aide support to assist them in the classroom or to help fund different schooling scenarios. I could not have navigated through this without the support of EPIC.

But emotionally, it was me who had to move forward from this. It was not Zalie and Flynn that got upset as much as I did. As a parent of children with additional needs when you lose one of your supports, there is a period of grieving and worry. With the hope that you can move forward to tackle the next challenge without that support. For many years, Chris was just a phone call away if I ever needed her and still to this day, she is aware of the twins' movements due to our access to social media.

It was May in the year the twins started three-year-old pre-school that I found out I was pregnant again.

I had always wanted four children, so I was excited but also nervous. We had our hands full at that stage, with a five-year-old and two three-year-olds. However, we felt that we could manage another little bundle of joy, and deep down I was hoping for a little girl so that Zalie would have a sister.

Early scans confirmed I was not having another set of twins, which would have been tricky.

So very blessed we were that following February, exactly three weeks after the twins' fourth birthday, that our second daughter, Anaye, was born.

She was perfect and I think she knew Mum and Dad already had a lot going on, so she was a very easy-going and relaxed baby.

It was wonderful to see the twins' interaction with their new baby sister. They were gentle and caring. Zalie in particular adored Anaye. She was besotted by her perfectly round little head and tiny feet and hands. It was so special to see Zalie cuddle Anaye and want to help me look after her. Though we had worried an extra baby might be too much, she was not a challenge.

Zalie took on a little mothering role and I began to see a different side to her, the compassion and joy she had being around her baby sister was beautiful to watch.

Flynn and Zalie, age – 4 years, with baby Anaye

Autism doesn't come with an instruction guide, it comes with a mother who never gives up.

CHAPTER 6

Will Give Anything A Go

When the twins were first placed in the spotlight, it became clear that things were going to be a little different in our family. I wanted to give them every opportunity to shine. I did not want those curtains to close, for them to be placed back in the dressing room and not given their moment on stage. What I mean is I did not want them to be overlooked in life; I wanted them to be accepted for who they were, but I needed to help them sort out issues that were holding them back.

We had behavioural problems, sleep issues, food intolerances or refusal to eat and communication difficulties. There were many things that we needed to work on. It was always one step at a time, but it often became overwhelming. Through these challenges, we spoke to different people to see what was working for them so we could get ideas and suggestions.

I went down several different pathways trying to make a difference, I was prepared to change things to see what would work for us. I had both Zalie and Flynn tested for coeliac disease at a young age which came back negative.

I knew from having a strong interest in natural therapies myself that you are what you eat, as the body works best when it is well-nourished and fed things that agree with you. I also knew the importance of working with your own special uniqueness to create a happier you. When your digestive system is going well you operate better. This means you are calmer and more able to focus on other things in life.

I could see that the twins, particularly Zalie, were possibly having a problem with their gut. Any imbalance in the gut affects the brain function and overall health.

This is also what I was reading, those on the autism spectrum are more sensitive to things. This related to food, certain clothing on the skin, bright lighting, loud noises and busy places.

I decided to focus on their health, their internal health, hoping it would make a difference to their overall well-being and therefore their behaviour, tolerance and understanding of the wider world and communicating with people.

Will Give Anything A Go

Our first interaction was with a naturopath who specialised in autism when the twins were two to three years old. He had a good reputation and a lot of experience working with dietary issues and children on the spectrum. He also had a network of people he worked with in the US that kept him up to date with new findings and ideas in these areas.

He was not ridiculously expensive, and we had some skin tests and hair samples taken and sent away to determine food allergies or sensitivities. The results came back stating that Zalie had an intolerance of almonds, cashews and blueberries, while Flynn's body did not like kiwifruit.

So, this was helpful. It was a start, and I found over time that getting a little bit of information from a variety of different people I came across or was introduced to helped me build up a bit of a food profile for the twins.

Apple juice seemed to make them a bit hyperactive, though they liked it, and so they were much better off drinking small amounts of a good quality orange juice.

I really opted to give them water, by choice, which is our bodies' preference, as we are 70 per cent water. I never allowed soft drink in the house, unless it was for a birthday party.

Actually, all four of my children were never given fizzy sweetened drinks, which was really interesting to see that when they went to a friend's home or to a party, their preference was still to ask for water. As soon as they tried soft drink, they could not drink it. The taste of sugary lemonade, Coke or Fanta was something they were just not used to and, in the end, didn't like, which was great. This would, of course, change as the teenage years came along.

When Zalie was three-and-a-half years old, I took her to see a kinesiologist. They work with movement, muscle monitoring and look for imbalances that may be causing problems in the body. Often children with autism are not as strong in their muscle development.

Zalie had trouble holding a pencil or crayon properly and was not using her upper body to its best ability. Plus, her attention span was so minimal, she was easily distracted and often just zoned out, like she was in another world.

Prepared to give things a go to better Zalie's life, I had been recommended to a kineseologist on the other side of Melbourne. So, I took Zalie one weekday for an afternoon drive.

At the time, I was actually in the early stages of my pregnancy with Anaye.

We entered his rooms and had a good chat, he seemed very experienced and discussed his process, to best assist Zalie. It would mean she would have to lie on the therapy bed and he would work with her muscle movement and put her in a relaxed stage to be properly assessed. Well, this lasted about two minutes. Zalie, being the sensory girl she was, would not have a bar of some male she did not know attempting to work with her body, even a touch of a leg muscle. It became apparent quite quickly that this may have been a waste of an afternoon drive and money as Zalie was simply getting quite upset and confused, we had tears. Then I was getting upset. This was not a process you could explain to a three-year-old, particularly when communication was not her strong point. However, it was then suggested he could use me as a surrogate by working on my muscles with Zalie in the room, while she was kept occupied. At the time, this did test me – really, I was finding this hard to understand, was he serious? However, knowing we had driven all this way and I would still have to pay for the session. What harm could come from it?

Well, I was surprised. As I laid on the therapy bed, I told him I was pregnant. Zalie was agitated but holding a sensory squeeze toy with one hand and my hand with her other. As he began working on me, she actually started to relax, her body calmed, she sat down and appeared to go into thought. Zalie and I both left that session feeling quite calm, and he suggested moving forward that he could assist Zalie by working on her while she was at home, that the surrogacy could be done remotely also. This, I was not so sure about, and felt that moving forward we would just find someone who lived closer to our home. However, the whole experience was very enlightening, and once again I gained further understanding of Zalie and her capabilities. She was very in tune with her body and our world in a way that was different to my experience.

A gluten and dairy free diet (GF/DF) was all the rage at the time. Often referred to as the GF/DF diet, this eating plan avoids foods that contain gluten (found in many breads and cereals) and casein (found in milk products). It was suggested that eliminating gluten and casein may help to change symptoms and behaviours of autism. Many people that we chatted to were trying this eating plan out on their child with autism. We substituted rice or almond milk for cow's milk, tried soy and used a lot of rice-based products instead of wheat.

Although the twins had been tested for coeliac disease and the results came back as negative, it was still suggested by our naturopath and dietitians at the time that giving this diet a go, taking things back to basics, could possibly lead to some positive changes in their behaviour. I did hope it would not be a long-term plan as avoiding many breads was not easy or cheeses, even ice-cream as a treat. After several months, I did notice some slight changes in behaviour, which was positive. However, the selection of food was tough for the twins. The gluten free bread available when they were five and six years old, was not of a great or tasteful standard; it was dry and bland.

I was baking biscuits and tried making my own breads, but it was hard going, when you had four young children and the busyness of life. I felt it was only logical to once again pool all of the information I had gathered from trying something else and slowly introduce back certain foods and see how we went. Plus, I was also concerned about providing a complete balanced diet. We always stuck with our organic fruit and vegetables, which avoided the nasty wax from supermarket bought apples or chemical sprays. So, I was doing the right thing there, but I wanted them to be happy when they were eating also, and they were not happy on a GF/DF diet. However, I do have several friends that found such a great improvement in their children's behaviours, focus and overall wellbeing that they have stayed on this diet.

I learnt to do everything in moderation. Bake your biscuits and slices to avoid the additional additives which only create hyperactivity in children, avoid white breads and rolls, eat plenty of fruit and vegies, limit soft drinks only to special occasions if at all. They loved a Milo with milk, but I just wouldn't give it to them every day. It was all common sense, really.

What I did learn which was of great help to Zalie, who seemed to be more affected by standard cow's milk than Flynn, was the benefits of goat's milk. Zalie was not partial to rice, almond or soy milk, as everyone is different, however goats' milk she enjoyed. Although it is more bitter than cow's milk, it is also more easily digested by the human body. Once again, we keep it minimal. I introduced more nuts and legumes into the twins' diets. They both loved chickpeas, as I discovered.

We had a lot of food avoidance and food tantrums when the twins were younger, such as not wanting to eat if there was something green or orange in the meal. For many months, there was a lot of white on the plate. But being a naturally healthy eater myself and encouraging it in all my children. I persisted with the twins, it wasn't easy to negotiate, but we found a way, using our PECS: if you eat this, you will get this.

It is a form of bribery, but it seemed to work. As parents we were prepared to do whatever it took to get the twins to keep trying foods. Like any mum, I would attempt to hide finely chopped vegetables in the Bolognese sauce.

There were nights, I won't deny that when I was at the end of my tether and felt like crawling into a ball and going to sleep. But a negative mealtime was not pleasant, so I would do whatever I could to avoid this. It was always nicer to sit down as a family and eat, but some nights, if it meant someone was quietly doing a puzzle while eating dinner or drawing, then as long as they were eating, I had to accept that it was OK!

When Flynn was younger, he suffered from eczema then asthma. Both are linked to inflammation. Research suggests that if you have one condition you are more likely than most people to have the other. Not everyone with asthma has eczema, but there is a strong link. Flynn's eczema was annoying and the asthma, fortunately, was not severe, but enough that he needed to take a puffer with him when out or at school and had a preventor at home. I did truly hope it would only be childhood asthma.

Our dietitian suggested that I try a diet that cut down on salicylates, to see if this would assist the eczema, and possibly the asthma, and that it would not do Zalie any harm to try this also. Salicylates are natural chemicals made by plants, found in fruits and vegetables.

There are natural and synthetic forms (such as in toothpaste and food preservatives) and they can cause adverse reactions in some people. It was easier to introduce across the whole family, particularly at mealtimes, while snacks were best sorted individually. We used leeks instead of onions, maple syrup instead of honey and margarine was replaced by Nuttelex. There were various easy alterations that we have stuck with, even to this day. I found it quite easy to make simple changes that did not greatly affect what we ate as a family. I did stick with this diet strongly for many months and experimented with different meal combinations and monitored the outcomes as best I could. I did notice a difference in Flynn's skin and fortunately he was a child that grew out of the eczema and asthma. Zalie just seemed calmer overall.

Once again, I felt here that trying this gave me further insight into what foods worked best for the twins and what combinations were not too difficult for me to manage when preparing meals with a busy young family.

Our dietician has helped many times over the years. When the twins were younger, I discussed and recorded meal schedules with him documenting what was eaten, over a day or two and what reactions I sighted after the food was consumed. He is a strong believer in gut-brain balance, which I also truly appreciate. If your gut is happy, digesting well and in balance, then the brain function will be at its optimal performance. Having good gut bacteria is very important for overall health and wellbeing.

There is definitely a strong gut-brain connection in children on the autism spectrum and something I felt as a mother to twins with autism spectrum disorder (ASD) I needed to help manage for them. It is not something they could monitor or understand themselves, and I only hoped that one day the time would come, as they grew into teenagers and young adults that they would start to understand and appreciate what foods worked for them, what made them feel good within themselves and how it affected their ability to function to their best capabilities.

*If you have met one person with autism,
you've met one person with autism.*

– Dr Stephen Shore

CHAPTER 7

The School Run

Every morning in that first year of school the bus would arrive at the front of our house and the twins would very happily jump on board and head off for their day, with smiles on their faces. This was such a relief each morning, as there was an assistant on the bus, who I could communicate with regarding any morning issues before school. Zalie often got travel sickness and preferred to sit at the front of the bus. The bus would also bring the twins home again in the afternoon. It felt safe and secure, and it was a routine we all adapted to quickly. It gave me time to focus on getting Bryce and Anaye ready for their day, once the twins were on their way. I could then drive or walk Bryce to school and spend one on one time with Anaye.

Flynn would be dropped at Montmorency Primary School, and Zalie at DVSDS in Greensborough. They were both aged five years and found the days tiring in the beginning.

As they were both still very limited with their verbal ability, I did not get a big rundown of the day's events when they arrived home after school or that night while sitting around the dinner table, like I did from their older brother, Bryce. This can be very hard for a parent to deal with, you naturally want to ask questions and get answers about their day, even talk about feelings at different times during the day when things happened, or who they chatted to and played with.

The schools addressed this as best they could to support parents by sending home a communication book that the teachers could write in to discuss matters with parents and parents could write back. We also received timetables and regular photos of special moments or events. The teachers were also very happy to chat on the phone after school and at regular parent-teacher interviews. The twins' PECS communication folders were expanded with additional pictures from school, so they could be used to request things at school and to share things when they got home.

Flynn's Early Schooling

Flynn was accepted beautifully by the other boys in his class and by his teachers, and being at a mainstream school, he got to interact with other students and older students in Grades 4 and 5 who would come into their small class and help out with the students. They joined in on school sport days and book dress up days. They even did excursions together.

The School Run

Flynn absolutely thrived in this school environment. He had a teacher and an aide shared by five students in the class. All of these boys were on the autism spectrum, some were more verbal than others or slightly better at writing or reading, but generally they were all striving for the same thing: a pre-prep year to help them prepare to start a prep year at their chosen school.

As the year progressed, Flynn became less reliant on his PECS communication system and more confident in structuring basic sentences and conversation himself. His handwriting progressed, he could write his name and there were words and basic sentences being written and a small reader was coming home a few nights a week for him to attempt to read to his family at night.

Flynn fell into the school routine very well, and to this day, 13 years later, he still remembers the houses he would go to each morning and night on the bus to pick up his pre-prep year school friends.

One of Flynn's strengths is his amazing memory for people and places. When returning somewhere many years later he will still remember people and their names, or something he did while he was there.

He is the one I ask at home about an event we did as a family to jog our memories: 'Flynn, do you remember what happened when we were there?' He is always the one who recalls it.

Zalie and Flynn, age – 5 years, with Bryce

There was a lot of kindness at this school. Being very small in numbers, it truly had a friendly, nurturing environment, which is what Flynn needed for his first year. School days are long for a five-year-old. As Flynn was picked up and dropped off by the bus each day, I did not really get the parent social interaction that is usual. However, I did go by at least one afternoon a week to collect him for his weekly speech class, so in doing so I got to see the school and what was happening in the classroom. I was always greeted by the principal. Usually, I had Anaye in tow, who was a feisty one-year-old and she loved seeing her big brother at school.

Flynn continued to enjoy his weekly swimming lessons, one day a week after school. Zalie would also attend at the same time and they were now in separate classes based on their skill level. Swimming classes were very small so as to give each of the students personal attention.

The School Run

That first year of school, pre-prep, was wonderful for Flynn, as it gave him that in-between step. Not being ready for a mainstream prep class, but past what kinder could offer him. I will forever be grateful for the opportunity this programme offered Flynn. His personality was beginning to really shine through, and the teachers adored him. Regardless of all the things that were more difficult for him, and at the forefront of that were the social and communication aspects, he still always made an effort to say hello to people and was very kind to other students, even if often the conversations were really difficult for him.

The students were also supported by speech and occupational therapy staff, even though they were in a base room setting located at a different school away from the main campus of DVSDS.

So, you can imagine that, as the year came to a close, it was really difficult to let go of this very nurturing environment and making the decision to leave the school altogether was not easy, but it was only a one-year programme. A couple of the boys from Flynn's class were going to progress to the mainstream prep class at the same primary school. However, it had always been my hope that Flynn would attend the same primary school as Bryce. Eltham East Primary School was a much larger school and usually had four prep classes with 18-20 students. Plus, I felt that going to school with your big brother would be so very important for family unity, socialising and ensuring Flynn was happy and supported at school.

Zalie's Early Schooling

In Zalie's first year of school she was blessed with the most amazing teacher, Kathy, who, with a class of six students and an aide, went beyond the call of normal teacher duties. It would be nothing for Kathy to phone you in the evening after dinner to tell you of a special moment or achievement of Zalie's that particular day if she had forgotten to write it in the communication book. This was so reassuring as a parent that Zalie was being given every opportunity to be the best she could be every day at school with fantastic support.

It took Zalie more time to settle than Flynn and she found the days very long. Zalie had the opportunity to go horse riding every Wednesday at school in a highly supervised setting. There would be an assistant each side of the horse and an instructor leading the horse, for complete student safety. Zalie loved these sessions and it was my first opportunity to really appreciate the benefits of animal therapy for the calming and joyful effect it had on Zalie.

It certainly was not a year of all roses though, we had many hurdles to jump, particularly in regards to behaviour, and having an understanding of things that other families would consider to not be an issue.

Kathy and I worked so very well together to follow through every day in the classroom and continued this at home. Zalie's progress with her PECS communication was consistent and we were always working towards, reducing pictures and encouraging independent speech.

The School Run

In order for me to visit Zalie at school, to drop off an item she had left at home or attend a school function during the day. Between Kathy and I, we had to devise a visual communication strip and routine so that Zalie would not get anxious and upset, which brought on tears and frustration for her. In Zalie's eyes, if Mum attended school at any point, that must mean she would be going home, regardless of whether it was 11 am or 1 pm. Over the period of a month, of me visiting then quietly exiting the room when Zalie was occupied after a brief goodbye, she began to accept this and started to calm down. Zalie, I would learn, was a very routine girl – she could adjust to change but there had to be pre-warning of this, always with visual communication to back up verbal explanation. Zalie would just get lost with words, as they would enter her head and become twisted and confused. When you spoke to Zalie in those younger years, you could see she would only pick up on one or two words in a sentence when spoken to, so she would often misinterpret what was requested meaning visual communication support was always needed.

Zalie completed her first year of school at DVSDS and her progress with communication, speech, receptive language (her understanding of what others were asking her to do) and in particular, behaviour was such that she would move the following year into a base room scenario. We could not have been prouder of her. This had been a year of hard work from her teacher Kathy and myself at home, a credit to everyone, but most of all to Zalie.

Similar to Flynn with his pre-prep programme, Zalie would be going to Briar Hill Primary School, still under the guidance of a Special Developmental School, but mixing daily with the students at Briar Hill Primary. Her class would also have a teacher and an aide, shared by six students, and she would be given the opportunity to sit in weekly on play sessions with mainstream prep classes and have guidance and interaction with Grades 4 and 5 students who would assist in the special needs class at their school. Briar Hill Primary was a small school with a Steiner stream, so they had chickens in the playground and a very nurturing, artistically focused environment.

Out of the school environment, Zalie began dance lessons at a local dance studio. Like any little girl, Zalie loved to dress up in her dance clothes and a tutu. At home, she would always be running around in a costume, whether it was a fairy dress or a Tinkerbell outfit.

Over time, Nicole, her dance teacher, who ran The Edge Performers School, could see Zalie needed support, so she suggested one of the older students from another dance class attend class with Zalie to help assist her to understand the dance moves and guide her. This gave me the opportunity, like any other parent, to be able to sit back and enjoy watching my daughter dance and Zalie was also able to participate in the end of year concerts, often with her dance assistant also on stage, which was wonderful for Zalie's self-confidence and for us as a family to be able to watch her.

Both Zalie and Flynn enjoyed trying new activities, but they always participated in individual activities in those early years. Team sports were too hard for them to understand and get used to. There was too much going on, too many voices, too busy. Individual sports like gym classes or tennis lessons worked well. One-on-one scenarios, where the instructor had time to communicate and understand how to explain things, were their best opportunities to learn new things.

It became obvious early on that hand-eye co-ordination and fine motor skills for both the twins were not as developed as other children for their age. It would take longer for them to learn to write and to be confident to catch a ball or hit a ball with a bat or racquet or kick a football.

Team sports were off the radar for many years. But all in good time.

As that first year of school came to a close for the twins, I looked back at all our achievements. I was very emotional to be leaving such supportive teachers and programmes, but so proud that the following school year as two six-year-olds – Flynn would be starting at Eltham East Primary School, a mainstream prep student, with his big brother Bryce in Grade 3 and Zalie would be attending school 10 minutes' drive away at Briar Hill Primary School, also a prep student in a mainstream environment. Anaye would be a cheeky, but very mature, two-year-old at home with her mum.

Fast Forward a Few Years

Up in Lights

It is typically the case that siblings within one family will go to the same primary school.

Lovely moments are shared walking to school and attending school functions. For our family with four children and different circumstances, we spent many years at four different schools. Being various combinations of primary, secondary, special schools.

Rainy day mornings were a nightmare. However, there was only one year, in 2012, when we had all four children enrolled at the one primary school.

This came about when Flynn was in Year 3, Bryce in Year 6, Anaye had started prep and Zalie was attending the mainstream primary school, Eltham East, one day per week on a dual placement enrolment. Dual placements are very common for families who have children with ASD. Attending a specialist setting for learning, but to expand social skills and for family unity, attending a mainstream setting with their siblings.

I really enjoyed that one day a week, it was a Monday, we all walked or drove to school together. All in the same school uniform, feeling like every other family. Due to Zalie's social and academic skills not being as strong as Flynn's, she was placed in the Year 2 class one day a week. The other students really enjoyed having her in the class, particularly the girls and she had an aide for the day, Vicky, who was very supportive.

Flynn, Zalie, Bryce, Anaye

It was during this year that the school held their bi-annual concert. It was a big event, involving months of planning and rehearsals for the 600 plus students, and an audience of over 1500 family and friends. It was held on stage at Monash University. Children had to audition for speaking parts and there were costumes to be made. For our family, there was an opportunity to have four siblings on stage together for the only time in their life, participating in the one school production. Vicky and I asked the school if Zalie could participate, although she only attended one day a week, as it would mean so much to our family, for her to get this opportunity. It was agreed she could. We knew it would be challenging for both Zalie and Flynn, learning the dance moves and being on stage in front of hundreds of people with lights and music, but they were both keen to give it a go. It was not an easy decision for the school, such was the pressure felt to have a smooth-running production, there was an element of uncertainty whether Zalie could manage, the rehearsals, the show, the late night. She had participated in very small school productions but nothing on this scale. It did take some convincing, but then everyone was on board and it was full steam ahead. Zalie needed to be given that opportunity – yes, it would be challenging, but what an achievement if it went well.

As the opening night came closer, there was no more we could do; both Zalie and Flynn had their respective costumes, they had rehearsed and visited the venue. Vicky had volunteered to be backstage with Zalie during the evening, to keep her calm if need be. Our family and friends were in the crowd and I could feel the buzzing anticipation and excitement in the large concert hall. I was so excited but nervous for the twins that I think I literally held my breath for most of the production.

Anaye in prep had auditioned and been given a speaking role, so she came on first and was adorable in her part on stage surrounded by the gorgeous prep students. Zalie entered next with the other Year 2 students, playing the role of a teddy bear and was required to begin her scene lying on the floor with another student who was her helper for the night on stage. Her helper lay next to Zalie, also dressed as a teddy bear. The stage was dark and as the music began, they were to rise at the right moment and begin their dance. I still recall the look of shock in Zalie's eyes, as the lights came on and she peeked up and got a glimpse of 1500 people, eyes fixed. I was so nervous for her and so was Vicky backstage. But she did it, she followed the other students and with only one little noise out of cue, her moment was done. I think even the school principal was proud and relieved that evening. Zalie's achievement was a credit to everyone who had helped her. She did it! Flynn was on next and he showed such enthusiasm performing his part that I could not take the smile off my face and he did not appear nervous at all, but was running on adrenaline with excitement. Every movement was over emphasised, why not, everyone's watching, let me shine, he must have thought.

Bryce was on next, in his final year of primary school, and he just grooved along. I think he was just glad it was over, and the four of them had all done so well.

Sometimes it is the people no one can imagine anything of who do the things no one can imagine.

– Alan Turing

CHAPTER 8

Those Moments

This journey for Zalie and Flynn is ongoing, as autism is something you have for life – it does not go away, there is no cure. Your brain is wired differently. So many things are possible if you are taught the right way, given the opportunity and are never told you can't.

I have never given up. Like any mum, there are moments when I have wanted to. Plenty of nights I have just laid in bed and cried. Cried in that moment, cried for the future. I cried because I have wanted to run away. But it is the moments of achievement, when something just clicks and all the hard work has paid off, that keep me going.

Flynn and I were driving into the city one day as he had an appointment. It is always lovely to enjoy one-on-one time with your children, a chat in the car, a walk just the two of you. Giving them your full attention. Flynn was really starting to ask a lot more questions. In that eight-to nine-year-old age bracket he had started to gain more confidence with his speech and was generally showing a curiosity about things.

I have noticed over the years, with both Zalie and Flynn, that movement stirs up more thoughts and words, whether it be bike riding, driving in the car, horse riding. An interesting concept that I have read about also.

On this particular day, Flynn was chatty. A tram crossed our pathway while we were sitting at a set of traffic lights. It was a brightly painted tram, advertising and promoting the city, with the words, 'Come enjoy the City of Melbourne, Victoria.'

Flynn asked me, 'What do those words mean, Mum?' I simply explained.

We are driving into the city of Melbourne, which is in the state of Victoria, where we live. In the country, Australia. There are seven states within Australia. Melbourne is the capital city of Victoria, and every state has a capital city. The tram is promoting Melbourne to the people and visitors to come and visit and enjoy. I made a mental note to get the map of Australia out when we got home, as I knew it would be confusing for Flynn without a visual, to understand.

Flynn's response to me, 'Well, what's the lowercase city?' It took me a moment to understand what he said, and then it clicked. I just smiled and said, 'You are so clever.' That was

Those Moments

how he tried to interpret our conversation. I just loved in the moment how his mind worked. Then and there I learnt something new about my son, how he processed information. Could it not be logical that if you have a capital city, why could you not have a lowercase city?

It is a gorgeous story and I have mentioned it several times to people. I even entered those words and our conversation into a competition that an autism support group was running and Flynn won a prize.

Many of those special moments have been achieved and shared with other people who have come into our home to support our family. From as early as the twins were three years old, I was encouraged to reach out to the local council for assistance. This began with after school help. Carers, as we call them, who would come into our home under funding programmes. They would arrive after school, so that I may take Bryce or Anaye to an activity and not have to drag the twins along, or they would walk Zalie down to the park after school to play on the swing and blow bubbles while I cut up vegetables for dinner. They may spend time with Flynn in the backyard in the sand pit or doing his school reader while I folded the washing and did homework with Bryce.

It has made such a difference to our lives and you get to know people so well when they are in your home three afternoons a week. They become like family.

They have helped to teach Flynn how to finally tie his shoelaces after weeks of trying. Or there was the moment where we taught Zalie to tie her own hair up in a ponytail. While they might seem like simple things, they often take much longer for a child with autism to grasp, so the benefit of having community support is wonderful.

It has given balance to our home over the years and has enabled the demands of raising children with ASD to not always feel so intense.

What it has also taught Zalie and Flynn is resilience, that people can come and go in your life and it is OK. They may be there for a short or long while to help you at a particular stage, but when they move on it is OK. It has certainly been emotional at times, we have swapped gifts and hugs and wondered how we will cope now that a special person is no longer going to be in our lives. They have started a new job or made a career change, but we have always moved forward, knowing and hoping that someone else is just around the corner.

As autism is a social disability, communication is our greatest social asset. People with autism find communication hard, not knowing what to say at the appropriate times and having difficulty reading facial expressions. It does not come naturally to them. So, more often than not, it is easier not to talk, then you can't get it wrong.

In Zalie's case, she often preferred to put things into her mouth, rather than let words out. Her preference to taste things and test out the texture often meant a range of non-appropriate items, things you would not normally eat, such as playdough, plasticine or foil would end up in her mouth.

We have shared many positive and negative moments over the years based around communication. When Zalie was eight years old and in her dual placement school setting four days a week, she had two wonderful classroom teachers at Briar Hill Primary School, Fiona and Lisa, who were like joint second mothers as they knew her so well.

We were all concerned that Zalie had been complaining on and off for about two weeks of a sore ear. At that stage with Zalie, it was always hard to gauge how bad something was or the pain level, as her ability to explain with words was not strong. So, there was a lot of guessing. Zalie was prone to swimmer's ear, thinking it may be that; I had put in ear drops but it was not making any difference.

It was a Tuesday and I took her to the doctor who looked in her ear and said he could see a bit of wax build up, but nothing bad enough to warrant syringing the ear, which was something Zalie did not handle well. Flushing water into the ear canal played havoc with her sensory system so we avoided it where we could. The doctor said her ear looked a little inflamed, so he gave me some antibiotics and suggested I continue with the ear drops for another couple of days to try and loosen the wax. I was hesitant as Zalie did not enjoy the drops either. But I did as was requested. Zalie was still keen to be at school and was really up and down, one minute the ear was fine, the next not.

That same week on the Friday morning, Zalie was in class and suddenly was screaming in pain.

I was called to the school by Zalie's teacher, Fiona, and we rang the doctor, who could hear Zalie's screams in the background. Concerned about a burst eardrum, he suggested I rush her to the Royal Children's Hospital and he said he would call and tell them I was coming. Fortunately, I was home on my own and was in the position to do this. I rang Matt and told him to meet me there.

By the time we arrived at the hospital, Zalie was still in a lot of pain and was taken straight into the emergency department and a doctor found. After a quick consult with me and history given, they attempted to look at her ear, but she would not let anyone near it. She had to be sedated and was taken straight into theatre. Zalie has lovely small ears and ear canals, so it was not easy to see anything down them.

What they discovered was not a burst eardrum, but a small piece of foil and plasticine buried deep within Zalie's ear. Of course, the inevitable question arose as to how it got there. Wax had formed in front of these two items, which is why the doctor did not see them and as they were lodged in her ear, drops did not loosen them. Zalie must have been in more pain than she let on.

I was shocked. I knew Zalie enjoyed making things with her hands and would often place things in her mouth, but as for putting it in her ear, it was not something I had ever considered her doing or wanting to do. Furthermore, the fact that she could not tell anyone that she had done it was just as concerning. She made a full recovery and we lived on a heightened level of anxiety, every time we saw a piece of foil or plasticine in her hands, we watched her like a hawk. Just hoping she really had put two and two together and realised what had caused her so much pain. Her receptive language was fairly good, so we explained consistently why it was a big 'no!' to do it again.

What I did gain from this hospital emergency was the realisation that I needed to learn more about Zalie and what was going on inside her mind. I still felt like I did not understand her enough and how she saw the world from the inside looking out. Maybe speaking to teenagers or adults on the autism spectrum could be the answer, because in the future as Zalie moved through her teenage and young adult years, I needed to understand more to better support her. We still had too many barriers to break through.

Zalie, as I learnt from a young age, had a fascination for things in miniature. She would often stop to pick up very small things from the ground that other people would just walk over or look at a set of tiny teacups in a shop window.

The rainbow-coloured plasticine which had caused so much pain in her ear, she had begun to sculpt into little figurines, with amazing detail. A tiny *Alice in Wonderland* and white rabbit, a cowgirl with hat and boots, a ballerina.

Zalie had always enjoyed drawing, and her drawings were at her age level, but these sculptures were amazing. It really seemed to be another form of communication – when words were too hard, Zalie would talk by creating with her hands. Art, it seemed, was an outlet for her. It took her away from the busyness of daily life and the confusion of words could be expressed another way.

I started to place her sculptures into tiny black boxes hung on a wire to display them. A local secondary school was having an art show and running a primary school art competition as part of it. I rang the school and asked if Zalie could display her work in the primary section. There were guidelines as to what art could be entered – only drawings or paintings – but they were very interested in Zalie's story and her art and said she could have her own small table at the art show to display her sculptures. This was a wonderful opportunity. Zalie was only eight years old at the time and did not really understand what an art show was. It was exciting and we were a bit nervous, but on the night Zalie had her table with little black boxes and sculptures inside. We also displayed a small profile about her and her art. It gave readers an insight into her autism and art as a valuable form of communication for her. Zalie enjoyed wandering around looking at the primary and secondary school students' art and competition entries on display – plus eating the supper that was supplied.

Zalie received a lot of compliments and positive comments on her work that night. A well-known artist, Jenni Mitchell, was opening the evening and as part of her speech, she asked everyone to, 'Take the time to look at the tiny sculptures created by Zalie Copeland. The attention to detail and skill for someone so young was amazing.'

This came as a total surprise and was such a compliment to Zalie. Zalie was then called onto stage when the awards were presented and she received a Special Encouragement Award. We all thought it was wonderful, as Zalie could not technically enter the primary school art competition and it was the first time anyone had seen her work in public before. This was a beautiful moment for Zalie on stage at a secondary school in front of many talented teenagers, proud parents, teachers and the school principal. To be honest, I don't think that at her age and stage, she fully understood the significance of that moment for her art and how it would shape her in future. It gave me the positive reassurance that I was not just a proud mum, Zalie actually had a talent with art. Was creativity her thing?

It was not just Zalie who was showing her creative side. By this age, Flynn had moved on from his interest in trains and was enjoying cars, particularly the popular movie at the time, *Cars*. Flynn really loved to draw, and it is very common with children with ASD to get quite fixated on a particular thing or interest. Flynn felt he could relate to the characters in the Pixar film franchise, *Cars*, because the cars had faces – Lightning McQueen was his favourite – just as the trains in the *Thomas the Tank Engine* TV series had faces. Flynn's drawings of Lightning McQueen were so good, he would take them to school and show friends or draw them while at school. It was obvious that Flynn also found art an outlet to express himself and communicate.

Stop thinking about normal... You don't have a big enough imagination for what your child can become.

– Johnny Seitz

CHAPTER 9

When Someone Changes Your Life

Mothers of Daughters with Autism (MODWA) was formed by myself and a friend. It was a group of mums whose daughters ranged in age from 8 to 12 years. We decided to form our social group as there are far fewer girls on the autism spectrum than there are boys.

This group was a positive experience for our girls to meet and enjoy activities together while the mums connected and shared knowledge, experiences and company. We would try and meet monthly at a park or someone's house. We also went on outings to the movies, museums, horse riding. We shared a couple of years of social connection and for our daughters, who found making friends harder than other girls, it was a calm non-judgemental environment, you could be yourself. Zalie enjoyed these catch-ups, but, like any social gatherings, she was always happy to return home at the end. Her attention span, interest and social tolerance had a time limit. After a while, she would naturally retreat and do her own thing which I just had to accept. I hoped, in time, as she got older and her knowledge of social situations and how to play the social game would progress and she would be able to be involved for longer.

It was at one of our gatherings I mentioned I was looking for an adult, hopefully a female with ASD to help me understand, connect with Zalie better – possibly a mentor. One of the mums suggested I contact Donna Williams, an autism consultant. Having not really made any contact with adults on the autism spectrum before, this was helpful to have a recommendation. I had attended a couple of autism conferences, so was expanding my knowledge and network.

I first met Donna in her home and found out what an interesting, well-travelled, intelligent woman she was. She explained to me her background and the challenges she had faced, and I was truly impressed with what she had overcome to be who she was today. An author, artist, public speaker with ASD who held university degrees and did not speak until the age of nine. Donna said she would be happy to meet with Zalie and give me some guidance and her insight into how Zalie's mind worked, and what it felt like to be her and see the world through her eyes. Donna visited Zalie at our home about two weeks later. They chatted and Donna played a game and did some art with Zalie. It was amazing how quickly she could see things that were going on with Zalie, that I was just not aware of.

Donna asked me if Zalie ever sometimes calls people close to her by the wrong name, people she sees often, who may be of similar height and hair length. I said that sometimes she calls me 'Fiona', who is her classroom teacher, or she may call her teacher, Fiona, 'Mum' by accident in class. Donna said, 'I think Zalie is face blind' (prosopagnosia). I had not heard of this before and at first found it hard to understand. I knew she could see people and calling someone by the wrong name is something we all do. Donna felt that when Zalie looked at you, initially there was an element of confusion on her face and she really had to stare hard. But it was actually her art, the miniature sculptures she had been making from plasticine, which confirmed it. Whenever she made a person, the only thing they had on their face was a nose – but it was a strong definite nose, and there were no eyes, no mouth, no other facial features. Zalie was telling us through her sculptures that when she looked at people's faces, the prominent feature was a nose and the rest, I think, was somewhat of a blur. This would cause confusion in facial recognition. Donna's observation seemed to be correct, that Zalie was face blind. As she was only eight years, she could not verbally explain what she was seeing but I hoped she may be able to develop this ability as she got older.

Zalie always seemed to be content on her own, whether she was drawing, playing in the sand pit or doing a puzzle. She was not a child that actually needed to be playing with a friend or even next to someone to be happy. I had always thought it was because she had autism. However, Donna told me that if you take away the autism diagnosis, Zalie naturally has an autistic personality, as she is very comfortable in her own company. She also observed that, to Zalie, people passed by like they were trees. It was not her natural instinct to stop and talk and try and make a social connection. Walking past a person was no different to walking past a tree. Zalie would have to be taught social skills from a young age and she would need ongoing social support as she approached her teenage and young adult years, whereas to most children this comes naturally with age and social interaction. This did concern me at first, but over time I just hoped that this would lead to Zalie becoming a confident and independent adult, happy within her own self.

Over the few visits we had together, Donna explained a lot about Zalie, making different observations, and she introduced Zalie to coloured lenses that would be placed in glasses. Sensory overload for those with autism can be strong and at times too much. Coloured lenses could calm the effect of light, tones and strong colour. Donna wore coloured lenses and she had a range of them for Zalie to try and see which suited her best. This was very new to Zalie. To determine what colours worked best for her it was simply a matter of trying the different colours on her eyes and observing her facial reaction to what she was seeing and we did manage to get a 'yes' or 'no' answer in regards to what colour she preferred. The lenses were made in the USA and sent to Australia and we had them put into frames here. Zalie chose purple and green tinted lenses and had two pair of glasses that she would alternate depending on her sensory needs that day. They were not for sight improvement like typical glasses, but to calm what Zalie's eyes were seeing and processing to her brain.

When Someone Changes Your Life

I was aware that Zalie had a lot of difficulty reading, writing and pronouncing words, which I assumed was due to her ASD. However, Donna told me there was more going on.

She believed Zalie was actually dyslexic and also had verbal dyspraxia. If you have autism you can learn to read and write, however if other issues are causing you problems it just makes it that much harder. I had heard of dyslexia before but was not actually sure exactly what it was and how Zalie could be assisted with this. It was certainly very helpful to be told this, but I needed to confirm and somehow have Zalie tested. It really felt like poor Zalie had been thrown up against another roadblock. I contacted the Alison Lawson Centre in Melbourne that offered dyslexia testing and therapy.

If Donna's observations were correct, it could really help Zalie with her overall communication, as well as give guidance and direction to her classroom teachers. After a couple of visits to the Alison Lawson Centre, it was confirmed Zalie did have dyslexia, but with the overlying autism it had gone undetected. It was wonderful to have this confirmed, so we could move onwards and upwards. We began a programme of weekly visits to the dyslexia therapist, and Zalie was given eye exercises to do daily at home, also specifically designed worksheets and readers for children with dyslexia.

In Zalie's case, the letters actually moved around on the page, sometimes she just saw dots rather than the letter, which made it difficult to form words and read them. The eye exercises helped, her eyes began to strengthen. As part of this I did take her to an autism trained optometrist also to check her sight. Which seemed to be fine. After eight months of dyslexia treatment, we had started to notice some significant improvements with Zalie's basic reading and also her writing. Her schoolteachers were also supporting her more as they now understood, and it was really making a difference to her confidence. She was now happy to sit at home of an evening and attempt to read the school readers sent home. Everyone in her support network was now on the same page.

If Zalie also had verbal dyspraxia, as suggested by Donna, this condition could be confirmed by a speech therapist. Verbal dyspraxia is a condition where children have difficulty making and coordinating the precise movements needed to produce clear speech with their mouths.

Zalie's overlying autism had delayed this diagnosis, although she had been seeing speech therapists regularly since she was three years old.

To explain how this affected Zalie, it was that there was a delay in the processing from brain to mouth. If you took the time to observe when Zalie was asked a question or was reading, her mind would be ticking over but the answer would not come out as quick as for you and I. More often than not, people would cut in and answer for her. I could see she would get frustrated with this, and often then found it easier not to talk at all. Not only that, but when Zalie formed her words, it was harder for her to get out the correct sounds as her mouth muscles used for speech were not as strong as in other children without the condition. Both of these things could be worked on, now that we knew what was causing her so much frustration with communicating. Ongoing practice with mouth exercises and speech sounds she struggled with would improve the strength of facial muscles. Allowing Zalie time to answer a question when asked or giving her extra time to pronounce the words she was reading would improve her confidence.

Donna also told me about the difficulty Zalie had with numbers at this young age; for example the number three was not the best way to represent this to Zalie, as she must see three dots with the three to understand what it means, four must be seen with four dots. Otherwise, these numbers just appeared as symbols on a page that meant nothing to her. At this point for Zalie, numbers were harder to comprehend than words, so we had a long way to go.

This new information I now had in regards to what Zalie was actually dealing with was at first quite overwhelming. When you are already juggling several balls in life and then a few more are literally thrown at you overnight, you just don't have enough hands. However, if I dropped all the balls now and did not at least try to juggle these new ones, then all the hard work we had put in up to this point would be gone.

I took Zalie and Flynn to several Sunday afternoon gatherings with other children on the spectrum at Donna's home. There was dancing, music, food, bubble-blowing and time spent in the garden just hanging out and feeling comfortable with yourself. Zalie was eight years old when she first met Donna, and she remained in Zalie's life until she left our world when Zalie was 14. Donna and Zalie shared a special connection. They understood each other on a deeper level. Donna was an amazing artist who saw a lot of young Zalie in herself. She really gave me hope for Zalie's future. To this day, Zalie still talks of Donna. Whenever she mentions emotions of sadness in her life, she talks of Donna's passing.

We will be forever grateful for the knowledge Donna shared and what she understood about Zalie. She really changed Zalie's situation and helped our family greatly.

Zalie and Donna

Why fit in when you were born to stand out?

– Dr Seuss

CHAPTER 10

Growing Up

Flynn

Flynn's confidence grew as he progressed through his primary school years. From Prep to Year 2, he had Anna as his classroom assistant. She was kind and nurturing and really helped him with his foundational skills. In year 3, the school approached me as they had interviewed a male integration aide who was studying to be a teacher. We all thought this would be really good for Flynn. Bearing in mind, a classroom aide does not just support one child but is there for them and to also support the teacher and the rest of the students in that class when required.

Eddie and Flynn worked well together. Flynn looked up to Eddie. He helped him not only with classroom work, but was there to assist Flynn to learn skills in PE classes and school sports days. Eddie attended school camps with Flynn and was a great role model for Flynn as he moved towards his secondary school years.

Flynn has always been a very popular boy amongst his peers, in the sense that everyone knows him. Flynn is extremely kind-hearted and genuine – what you see is what you get with Flynn. He is never mean to people or has ever bullied anyone. When someone is unwell or upset, Flynn will be the first to ask how they are. People stop to talk to him when he is out. He has grown into this person as he has matured.

There was only one time in primary school, when Flynn was in Year 2, where he was on the receiving end of a form of bullying. Bryce was in Grade 5 and a couple of Grade 6 boys were asking Flynn to say or do things in the playground, which were not necessary or made him look silly. Bryce told me and we took it to Flynn's then classroom teacher, who asked Bryce to name the boys to her. Bryce worryingly answered. The boys were spoken to and from then on they made no further contact with Flynn.

During his middle primary years, Flynn did become quite defiant at home when school was starting to get harder and when his peers were beginning to form stronger friendships. He would hide his concerns at school and try to fit in, which meant by the time he got home at the end of the day, he needed to release that bottled-up frustration. The result of this was dealing with an angry and tired boy after school, which was not pleasant. This is very common for those on the autism spectrum, trying so hard to fit in, to be like everybody else that often when they are home in a non-judgemental environment, they must release that tension. Joining Sea Scouts at the Cubs level helped Flynn to connect with peers who had similar interests and a group leader for guidance was helpful. We attended a few family camps through Sea Scouts, which Flynn really enjoyed.

It was towards the end of Grade 5 that the students voted amongst themselves who would be elected as the school leaders and captains for the following year in Grade 6. Each child who was interested in a school leadership position had to make a speech in front of their whole year level, teachers and principal as to why they would be most suited. Flynn came home and said he would like to try for school Environment Captain. This was a big step, but one we, as his family, along with his classroom teacher and teacher aide all supported. Why not? The Environment Captain was one role which would require Flynn to speak every Monday morning in front of the whole school assembly. Not all of the leadership roles required this. Flynn's speaking skills were certainly not his strong point at age 11, but he could be understood. We set to work helping Flynn prepare a speech that he felt comfortable with and could deliver confidently. He practised at home many times and the day came to speak in front of everyone. Parents were not allowed to attend, thankfully, as I would have been too nervous for him.

But what I did hear from his teacher that afternoon was that a huge cheer and round of applause erupted from students and teachers at the conclusion of his speech. They were all so proud of him for finding the confidence to stand up in front of over a hundred people and speak.

Flynn was then successfully voted in as one of the school Environment Captains in Grade 6. We could all not have been prouder of his achievement. When Flynn started as a prep student, seven years earlier, the only student with an aide, there was no way I could have pictured how far he would come. A school leadership position, that was amazing. This was such an achievement and a credit to all the hard work put in by his school support team, myself and the rest of his family, but mostly just Flynn himself. He has always tried to be the best he can. You cannot make someone naturally likeable, kind or friendly; it's in their making, their heart, and people see this with Flynn. Flynn has always found it harder to fit in, not because he wasn't liked, but knowing what to say in social situations does not come naturally to him. He has had to teach himself by observing other people.

As Flynn was coming into his final year at primary school, this would be the end of his time with Eddie and the nurturing, supportive environment he had been a part of for the last seven years. He spoke every Monday morning at assembly with the other school environment leaders.

Watching your child finish primary school is always emotional, and making the move to secondary can be scary. This is more so for families with children who have additional needs. You sometimes wish it could just stay as it is.

For Flynn to progress successfully to a secondary school environment, the school would need to have a strong integration aide support team and we would need to apply for funding for his aide support to continue into his secondary years. Entering secondary school with an aide takes some adjusting. There is a lot of peer pressure and insecurity amongst teenagers, as no one wants to stand out from the crowd. Many parents hope that by the time their child has completed primary school, they will no longer need an aide. It is not unreasonable to expect this progress, and there are also various secondary school options; mainstream and special schools. I could have sent Flynn on without this support, but he would have really found it difficult in his more academic subjects and this would have caused emotional and behavioural problems. Flynn was not suited to a special school, as he would have regressed socially. There is never an ideal perfect school; you just make the most of what you have in your local area or within reasonable transport distance.

There is also no guarantee your future secondary school student will get aide support either. You must apply for it. This was something I started working on not long into Flynn's final primary school year. New reports were needed from his speech therapist, a psychiatrist, the school psychologists, his Year 6 teacher was also asked to submit her observations in a written report. Input was required from his future school. The Department of Education did not hand over money easily.

Basically, you put forward a case painting a picture of the worst scenario possible without lying in regards to the student's behaviours, academic abilities and outcomes for them if they don't get aide support. You must push and have a committed team of people behind you to help you complete this paperwork, parents cannot do it on their own.

Fortunately for Flynn, we were successful in applying for aide support, which we were all very pleased about. It was also a relief for the school he would be attending, knowing they had the funding for aides to give Flynn the best education options.

I knew telling Flynn he would be starting secondary school with an aide in some of his classes would not really be what he wanted to hear, as he wanted to be more independent, however in the long run for him to be successful at school, it was the best way forward.

At around this time of transition, Flynn, aged 12, joined his first team sport: basketball. Not having been able to grasp the busyness and flow of being in a team at a younger age. It was wonderful to see he had matured and developed and was prepared to give it a go. The other boys in his team, all friends from school, were very supportive and the coach took just a bit of extra time to explain things to Flynn so he always understood what was expected. The first season his team made the grand final although they did not win. The other team, from the same area, also knew Flynn and that it was his first season, and he was yet to score a goal. Such a wonderful group of local boys from two opposing teams, united in the last five minutes of the game to allow Flynn a clear pathway to score his first goal. I don't think there was a dry eye in the basketball stadium that afternoon at the end of a great game. All the parents and coaches knew what had just happened. Though it was a grand final and his team did not win, Flynn's friends raised him up on their shoulders with cheers from the other team to acknowledge his first goal. It was one of the most special moments of sportsmanship I have ever seen. Flynn continues to enjoy basketball to this day.

One of the more difficult elements of secondary school is making social connections. Finding the right group of friends while trying to be your natural self is not easy. Teenagers can be cruel, judgemental and emotions and hormones can take over. Boys seem to find it easier than girls. Girls can really be nasty to each other, whereas boys tend to be a little more relaxed and chilled out.

Flynn found his earlier secondary school years, year seven and eight, a little trying – he changed friendship groups a couple of times and ended up receiving invitations to parties, but not as many as he would have liked. He would ask me sometimes why he was not invited. This can be hard for a parent to explain, let alone accept themselves. I tried to be honest. 'Maybe they had limited numbers,' I would say. Or I would tell him, 'Don't worry, you will be invited to the next party, it's OK.' I don't think any answer was ever good enough. However, things changed, and Flynn found as he got older and found a group of friends who were right for him that he was invited to parties and social gatherings. He became less worried about socialising, and fortunately was good at keeping himself busy with his own interests and hobbies.

The problem is that social media plays a big role in teenagers' lives and Flynn was no exception to that. You can see where your friends are at any time, if given access and also see who has been invited to things and who hasn't. It can really be destructive.

Flynn was very pleased, at age 15, when the local roller-skating rink, which he attended regularly enjoying a skate, offered him his first part-time job. Flynn and I approached them, saying he was looking for work. The manager already knew Flynn, his capabilities and so he gave him a job working one afternoon a week helping with the games on the rink and the cleaning up after guests had left.

Zalie

By the time Zalie reached Year 4 at primary school, aged 10, she needed a change. Her schooling situation no longer suited her and was not going to be the best way forward, so we needed to consider where she would be attending secondary school. She attended one day a week at the mainstream primary school that Flynn was at, but the social and academic gap between Zalie and the other students her age was becoming too wide. She was starting to feel uncomfortable, so her time there was done. At her base room setting she attended four days per week, she still really enjoyed it, however looking towards her future, she would not be attending a mainstream secondary school.

It was a big decision, but for consistency and progression, I thought it would be best to send her to a specialist setting that went right through to Year 12. By doing this, she could start to form some solid friendships and connections if she went in Grade 4. Convincing her new school that she was ready and capable took a bit of work, so she attended a few trial days to see how she would go. They were at first not sure whether this school was the right fit for Zalie, however she proved her capabilities, and her enrolment was accepted.

Zalie would be in a class that had 10 to 12 students with a teacher and aide, starting in their primary school section progressing to their secondary school on the same campus and going through to Year 12.

It was at this age that I introduced Zalie to horse-riding on a Saturday morning with Riding for the Disabled (RDA). We had been on a waitlist for a few months and a place had

Growing Up

become available at RDA in Warrandyte. Zalie had previous horse-riding experience from her very early primary years, but this was different – there was less support and more independence required. Zalie took to this straight away. She loved brushing the horses, patting their noses and seemed to feel comfortable riding again. Not only that but like movement in a car, the movement while riding a horse encouraged communication. Animals can judge character and sense a kind soul, and the horses seemed to recognise this in Zalie. Though she experienced some anxiety and nervousness in the beginning, she worked through this with the help of the RDA staff. She was happy to jump out of bed every Saturday morning to ride at 8 am, which showed her dedication and love of this time. Her chance every week to connect with a beautiful animal. Sharing early morning light and silence, it has taught her balance, patience, kindness and has been great for her core strength.

Nine years later, she still rides every Saturday morning without fail. I truly believe it has helped her to progress from a young girl into a young lady. Keeping something consistent in your life, when you do have autism is very important. It can help you ride out so many storms. And if that consistency can be with animals even better. They don't judge or look at you like you're different. They look within you.

Zalie has taken her horse-riding skills away from the Saturday morning environment, riding with Anaye and I while on holidays locally, in Margaret River, Western Australia and the Scottish Highlands. I am so very proud of her for this.

Education Support

When you see a challenge ahead it's natural to look for support. Support comes in many forms: social, emotional, physical and educational, depending on the circumstances.

When Zalie made her move to Concord School, it was a big change for her and she needed help to settle in. She was

Growing Up

a pre-teen and I really felt she had more to give; she still had very basic reading skills, poor concentration and she struggled with her co-ordination and reflexes at times. I was introduced to a therapist by the name of Margaret who ran a programme called Learn Easily. Margaret offered Educational Support giving an individual assessment and used therapeutic movements to work with her student's learning difficulties. Margaret brought it to my attention that Zalie was not using her right and left brain as she should. It took one very simple assessment for me to understand what this meant at the time. Zalie was given a large seashell to hold up to her ear and to listen to the sea, as I remembered doing as a child. A simple pleasure really, we probably don't do enough of anymore.

Margaret asked Zalie to hold the seashell to her ear. Zalie is right-handed and naturally picked up the seashell with her right hand, so you would think she would put the sea-shell to her right ear. However, each time we asked her to put it to her ear, she would reach across her chest and put the shell to her left ear, which really shocked me at the time. It was a bit of a wakeup call.

A moment where you think, wow! Is there is something else going on here that I am not aware of?

It was at that point that Zalie began weekly therapeutic sessions with Margaret. She began with basic sequential movement patterns that stimulated the base of the brain. It started with rolling in a straight line on the floor keeping her body aligned and progressed to crawling by placing one arm and leg diagonally opposite each other and passing a small bean bag back and forwards in a circle between her hands and behind her back. Many basic steps were retaught for co-ordination and balance that somehow Zalie had missed in her younger years, which made me as a mother think, gosh what had I missed. Margaret was now re-teaching Zalie by working with her brain to activate movement and balance sequences. Each session ended with a painting that calmed and relaxed Zalie.

Zalie had many learning difficulties, lack of speech, poor memory and concentration. She would get easily frustrated. This affected her motivation to learn, as it was so very hard for her.

Over time, I began to see a different child. I remember saying to Margaret, 'If we can get Zalie to read, that would be amazing.' The exercises were brought home and I would practise with Zalie daily. Margaret opened up new doorways for Zalie as she began to speak more, her writing became legible, her co-ordination improved, she began to read and want to read. Zalie attended this program for several years.

Zalie experienced such improvements, that come the time of Flynn's greatest challenge in progressing from primary to secondary school at age 12, he also began attending weekly sessions for education support with Margaret. Flynn's attention span increased and he could focus longer on schoolwork. His coordination and balance improved and he became more confident. The success for both Zalie and Flynn on this programme refuelled my determination to take each stage as it came and find the right support at the time.

Growing Up

Unexpected

The final day of Year 4 for Zalie was an emotional one. It was mid-December, the usual time when school ends and the summer holidays start. She had to say goodbye to Fiona and Lisa, her two teachers who she had been with nearly every day for five years. They loved her as much as she loved them. There were gifts shared and tears. Briar Hill Primary School Base Room had been wonderful for Zalie. But it was time for her to move forward, accept new challenges to realise her full potential.

It also happened to be the same day Bryce was finishing Year 6 at his primary school. A close friend was having an after-school party for Year 6 families and siblings and parents were invited.

It was a warm day, so we played with water bombs made from balloons the kids filled at the garden taps and enjoyed lots of party food. By about 5.30 pm Zalie, Flynn, Bryce, Anaye and myself arrived home tired and emotional. I recall the date being around the 17th of December, not far out from Christmas.

Zalie and Anaye wanted to have a sleepover on the couch in the lounge room that night as school was finished and they hoped to stay up and watch a movie. Zalie was 10 and Anaye was 6 at the time. It was special for me that the girls wanted to do something together on the last day of school as we wound into the festive season.

The next morning it was a Saturday and there was a relaxed feel in the house, as school was over. Anaye jumped onto the bed to wake me up with a cuddle. I chatted to her about how her night went sleeping on the couch with Zalie. She said it was fun, and that Zalie was still asleep. I thought, wow, she must be tired after all of yesterday's emotions, as Zalie was always the first one up in the house. We will just let her rest, I thought. Anaye and I continued to chat, then she said, 'Mum, I might go back to the lounge room and watch TV.' It was several minutes later she returned again and said, 'Mum, Zalie won't wake up and she is shaking.' 'What?!' I exclaimed, and jumped out of bed, running to the lounge room.

Zalie was lying in the foetal position on the sofa bed in her nightie convulsing, she was drooling from her mouth and her eyes were flickering, half open, half closed. It was the biggest fright of my life. I screamed out for Matt and we tried to wake her, but she would not come to and remained in the same state. We immediately called an ambulance, which took 20 minutes to arrive – the longest 20 minutes of my life. The paramedic injected Zalie with benzodiazepine to try and stop the seizure, while we waited.

After several minutes, Zalie appeared to be waking from the seizure and was unaware of what had just occurred. She seemed very tired and drained. Zalie and I then went via ambulance to the Royal Children's Hospital. This was Zalie's first seizure that we were aware of and it had lasted for 40 minutes, which is a very long time.

Zalie then spent three nights in hospital under strong observation to see whether she had any more seizures, and for testing. What was most concerning was that she had never had a known seizure and this one was so very long. It took a lot out of her.

Growing Up

There were a lot of questions asked by doctors and nursing staff and several tests done. Zalie did not have another seizure in hospital, and so we returned home and kept a very close eye on her. Fortunately, it was the beginning of the six-week school holiday, so she could rest and be watched.

Zalie returned to the hospital for check ups and was even monitored while sleeping. We were provided with medication to give to her in case she experienced another seizure. I had conversations with many people: doctors, specialists, other parents. Some of the suggestions given for why Zalie had this seizure included a one-off event or something which can occasionally occur in children approaching puberty or undergoing hormonal changes that can bring on a seizure.

She may never have one again, she may have one in 18 months, she may have one every month for the next two years – we would have to wait and see. We now had a plan to follow in case of a recurrence. Her schooling and social settings were all on the same page, with what the emergency plan was. At this stage, unless she had another seizure, she was not diagnosed as an epileptic. We worried, lost sleep, tried to figure out why it happened. Was it something she ate that triggered it, was she over-tired or emotionally exhausted? We tried not to wrap her in cotton wool, which is the initial, natural reaction.

Fortunately for Zalie, life went on as normal. That one long 40-minute seizure to this day is the only one she has ever had, thank goodness. To the point now that a decade later, we no longer highlight it as a medical concern, and for about five years now we have not carried the medication with her.

Losing the Rabbit

Zalie, at age 12, had to endure a personal hurdle that many pre-teens face: she really needed braces. For someone with a heightened sensory system and who did not like visiting the dentist at all, I knew this was not going to be easy for her. But to leave a pretty young girl, who already had her fair share of challenges, to deal with unsightly teeth for the rest of her life, in my opinion would not be right. I was adamant we needed to find a way to get Zalie through this. Fortunately, she had watched her older brother Bryce go through wearing braces, top and and bottom, so she knew what they were, and we had a starting point. I began by taking her to a couple of appointments with Bryce so she could meet Dr Sam, the orthodontist, and get comfortable with her and hopefully the surroundings of the orthodontist's rooms.

We had some X-rays taken, talked Zalie through standing still with her mouth secured on a piece of equipment to take photos and gave her time sitting in the orthodontist's chair and just letting Dr Sam look in her mouth. It was her top teeth that needed the work, as her bottom teeth were not that bad, so we would not need to put her through the trauma of both top and bottom braces, which was far more painful than a single row. Dr Sam said Zalie would get away with eight braces across her front teeth. This would still be a challenge. Now, Dr Sam is one very patient woman, dealing with teenagers and adults and the uncertainty and nervousness they feel around getting braces with the kindness and respect she does, takes a special kind of person. I hoped her and I working together could get these braces on Zalie.

Growing Up

When the day came, Zalie had been shown plenty of visuals so that she knew what was going to happen, but that didn't mean she was ready for the experience of having them in her mouth or having someone spend so much time putting them in. Holding her jaw open, the taste of the glue – there were many parts of this which she would find challenging and overwhelming. Dr Sam sat on one side, the dental nurse on the other, and me holding Zalie's hands so she would feel comforted and not push anyone away while the braces were being put on. It began OK, but by about halfway through, Zalie was no longer coping. She was really getting agitated and uncomfortable and having trouble keeping her mouth open. Dr Sam turned around to me and said, 'Joanne, I don't think this is going to work, we may have to stop.'

We had come too far and I was not prepared to let Zalie leave without braces that day, as I knew we would not have a second chance. So, I stopped the procedure and chatted to Zalie – bribery was needed. I promised her McDonalds on the way home, new art supplies, pipe cleaners, foam balls and the biggest canvas she wanted from the shop. I asked Dr Sam if I could be the dental assistant and if she would mind if I sat on Zalie's other side and helped with the final parts of putting her braces on. Dr Sam could see my determination and agreed. Together we did it – Zalie's braces were on. There was cheering and relief from all of us. We knew she could not take them off herself, and once the procedure was over, Zalie was much more settled, and she actually looked good with braces!

My philosophy is: It's none of my business what people say of me and think of me. I am what I am, and do what I do. I expect nothing and accept everything. And it makes life so much easier.

– Sir Anthony Hopkins

CHAPTER 11

On The Road

As Zalie and Flynn are both visual learners – most children on the autism spectrum are – they need to see and experience something to really learn, as doing the activity themselves and getting their hands dirty is what teaches them.

This extends into going places, experiencing a hot, sticky climate or ice-cold weather rather than just seeing it on television or hearing a story told to them.

For this reason, I have always encouraged travel in our family. The twins both first went on an aeroplane when they were two years old. They have been fortunate enough to have been to every state in Australia, cruised on a large ship to the South

Pacific Islands and have travelled to New Zealand, Indonesia, Japan, the UK and Europe. These opportunities have given them a better understanding of our country and the world. When I get out a globe of Planet Earth, and say, 'Remember this?', or how long that aeroplane flight took, they can visualise it or connect in their mind how long they sat on that plane for. We talk about the weather in different countries, the typhoon we experienced in Japan, the humidity of Darwin, how cold it was in the Scottish Highlands and the beauty of the Eiffel Tower in Paris. They both really enjoy train travel.

For our family, these experiences have created wonderful memories, but predominantly a greater understanding for the twins of what is beyond their everyday 10-kilometre radius.

I truly believe this type of education is just as good as what you get in schools, particularly for children who find school difficult; for those who cannot sit and write the thousand-word essay or do trigonometry. Travel, life experiences and meeting new people in different places are all different types of schooling.

I have found this to be the greatest education the twins could have had. Not only that, but it gives them conversation skills and something to talk about to other people. Autism can be socially very limiting, however travel is a conversation that unites us all.

Travel also gives you a sense of independence and freedom that those with ASD often struggle to find, even if you need the assistance to travel with a companion. You feel like everyone else when you are out there seeing the wider world.

As a family, we have made sacrifices to enjoy these travel opportunities – we do not eat out a lot at restaurants or have collections of material things. But in my opinion, travel and expansion of the mind are better ways to spend your time and money.

Travelling when the twins were younger took some organising. Limited time in transit was always best, so we tried to take the most direct plane flight and made sure to sit in the least noisy section of the plane. We ensured Zalie always had pencil and paper to draw with and negotiated with airlines to allow us to board the plane first to avoid heightened anxiety levels. The benefit of starting their travelling experiences at a young age has meant that as they progressed into their teenage years, they became more confident and comfortable with travel situations. Both the twins are better flyers than I am. They rarely get nervous. I will always continue to encourage travel for both Zalie and Flynn as they progress into adulthood.

It is this notion of travel and independence that brings you to the question of learning to drive. Where we live in Victoria, Australia, you are allowed to get a learner's permit at age 16. It is a natural progression for most teenagers to want to get their learner's permit when they turn 16 and for parents to be expected to start to teach them to drive or get the assistance of a qualified driving instructor.

For Flynn, watching his older brother successfully gain his learner's permit and then his full driver's licence at age 18 made him want to do the same, of course. He has always had an interest in trains and cars and has pictures of cars and motorbikes hanging on his bedroom wall. Going back a few years, if you had asked me when the twins were in Year 7 whether they would ever learn to drive, gain a learner's permit and eventually be on the road, my first reaction would have been wishful thinking of, 'Yes, I think Flynn will get there eventually,' and, 'Yes, I would love Zalie to get there also, but it is possibly just a pipe dream.'

For both to pass their tests, to cope with the pressure of being watched, the quick reactions needed, dealing with aggressive drivers, the list goes on.

But as you learn being a parent, one minute their toddler's turning five, next minute they are 12-year-olds turning 16. Time flies by. I have lived this journey always supported by a network of people including family, friends, carers. When you have ticked one box, one challenge sorted, there is always another one the next day.

It keeps you on your toes and always thinking. The day arrived when the twins were approaching 16 and Flynn, like all his friends at school, was keen – more than keen – to get his driving learner permit.

I have had my support coordinator, Narelle, working with me for many years now. When we switched over to the National Disability Insurance Scheme (NDIS) in Australia, Narelle who was already helping our family with carers came on as support co-ordinator to help me navigate two children through this new programme. We had to set up two individual plans as both Zalie and Flynn's needs were different and it was wonderful to finally have some financial support, as previously we had funded most of the speech classes, and therapies over the years on our own, which was not easy. The NDIS plan for an individual is reviewed each year and a new plan submitted, hopefully followed by an approval of the funding requested for the services required in the coming year. There is quite a lot of preparation before each plan review. Particularly when you are doing two. The upside is that a successful application to put the right plan and funding in place opened up many doors that following year.

I had been chatting to Narelle about Flynn's eagerness to try and get his learner's permit, and my concerns. Even the basic test, reading the book, understanding the technical side of road rules, was complicated for me, and I had been driving for 30 years! I struggled to comprehend how Flynn was going to pass this test without having ever been on the road, which he really needed as a visual learner. Narelle had come across a programme which assisted teenagers who had some challenges and struggled to pass their learner's tests. They taught you visually how to understand, answer and pass the questions. Rather than just being words and pictures on paper or a screen, they made it more hands-on by sitting you behind the wheel, taking you on the road and breaking down the questions for you.

What a great idea! This was in November, with the twins turning 16 in February the following year, and over those Christmas holidays during the six-week break from December-January, the Edge Community Services ran an intensive programme which required Flynn to attend a course one-and-a-half hours' drive away from home, five times over a two-week period. This, I thought, was doable. It was the school holidays, he could make the three-hour return journey in a day, and we would just have to do it five times. It would be worth it if by the end he passed his learner's test and gained his permit.

Apparently, they had teenagers who previously failed their learner's three times, but after doing the programme they had passed. Rather than put Flynn forward with the likelihood of failure, and all the emotions that follow. Doing this programme before he sat his test would be the best thing for him. It would give him confidence and understanding, and the teachers were trained to help, they even recommended that when the time comes, Flynn would sit for his learner's permit at the RTA just around the corner from where they were running the programme, rather than our local RTA near home. They were more understanding of children with ASD and gave them the time and space required to sit the test without stress.

Flynn was very keen to do the programme, regardless of the travel involved. After a discussion with Edge Community Services who ran the programme in regards to Zalie, they convinced me to also give her the opportunity to do the programme. Although at the time she was really not that fussed about learning to drive. The timing to attend this Driver's Ed programme suited us. Normally, they did not run an intensive programme and you had to attend during the school term one day per week. Being a one-and-a-half-hour drive from us, this was not really a great option. I was more than a bit concerned that Zalie was not ready, but thought I should not underestimate her, as she may enjoy it, and even if she didn't pass her learner's test at the end, she would have a better understanding of what was required in future. Also, the valuable advantage for Zalie, whose communication skills at that stage were not to the level of Flynn's, in having Flynn at the course with her was that he could help her if need be.

Fast forward to the completion of the programme in the January. The twins both gained a lot from the course, however

On The Road

they did not turn 16 until the 7th of February so we had three to four weeks before they could sit the test for their learner's permit. Now, if you don't practise, we all know that you lose what you have learnt. We then had the programme mentor, Dion, visit our house and work with Zalie and Flynn a couple of times and I sat with them online doing practice learner's permit tests over and over for the next few weeks.

On the day of their 16th birthday, I had booked them into the RTA in Geelong. We made a day of it, taking the time off school. We caught a train into the city and then jumped on the country train to Geelong, where they had done their driving programme. We had some lunch at a café nearby and Dion then picked us up in his car and drove Flynn, Zalie and I to the RTA.

Knowing how much information Zalie and Flynn were nervously retaining in their mind from doing the driving programme and the practice tests for a month, I was keen to get them both sitting for their test ASAP. I did not want them losing anything they had learnt. As we had now arrived at the end of the school holidays and they were both back at school, they had a lot going on in their minds already with starting a new school year. I think Dion and I were more nervous than the twins.

Flynn went in first with the tester and he passed with a score of 85 per cent. He was thrilled! All the driving and practice had been worth it and he passed the first time. It was then Zalie's turn, and honestly, I felt that this could really go either way. I knew they would be understanding and give her time, that they would rephrase questions if necessary, which was the reason we had travelled so far to this particular RTA.

She came out and I was holding my breath. The tester said she passed, also with a score of 85 per cent. I cried. It felt like a miracle. She did it! We took photos, holding up the permit passes and headed home on the train after all giving Dion a big 'thank you' for his support also.

I could not have been prouder of what both Flynn and Zalie had achieved. It just really showed that regardless of what your hurdles and limitations are in certain areas, if you are taught in a way that works for you, you can do anything. They were both proof of this. By putting in some hard work beforehand, they did not have to endure the pain of struggling to do this on their own, with a system of teaching they would not have coped with and had avoided the high likelihood of failure and sitting for re-tests. Now anyone who knew the twins at age 16, when I told them Flynn had passed, and then that Zalie had passed, their reaction was initially a moment of shock followed by a, 'Wow! Well done!'

Flynn took to driving like a duck to water – well, so he thought; he was very confident. It was a requirement for him to have an OT assessment prior to starting his lessons. It was decided to place him on a restricted learner's permit in the beginning. This meant he could only drive with a qualified driving instructor who had a dual controlled vehicle and was capable of working with learners who had ASD. This was for Flynn's safety and that of other drivers on the road, giving Flynn enough time to build up some basic driving skills. Fortunately, the NDIS, at my request, had added driving lesson funding to both Zalie and Flynn's plans. As each driving lesson with an instructor is just over $100, this was a big help.

After six months of lessons, Flynn was reassessed and his learner's permit restriction was lifted. From this point, he could continue lessons with his driving instructor, but I was also now allowed to take him for driving lessons. With his restriction lifted, he was now like any other learner on the road, which was a fantastic achievement at just 16 years and six months. It was great for his confidence to feel like every other 16-year-old boy he knew. Flynn enjoyed continuing to learn to drive and was very enthusiastic. When he turned 18 and had about 20 driving hours to go, he was picked up by the council funded L2P programme, a volunteer programme run by our local council where a trained volunteer mentor driving instructor is matched with a learner driver. This was a great opportunity for Flynn to experience driving with someone else who was not family.

Brad, Flynn's mentor, was very patient and helped Flynn to get all his night hours done to meet his driving requirements and really boosted Flynn's confidence by making sure he was fully ready to be tested for his P plates (probationary driver's licence test).

Flynn's day finally came to be tested for his probationary licence. He did not have to go down the usual road of a driving instructor through a local RTA. But was assessed by a Vic Roads registered OT assessor who had met Flynn before. This took away the issue of the unknown and the uncertainty of someone who did not understand Flynn being his tester for one of the most important moments of your life. The test was delayed a few times due to COVID-19 restrictions which was difficult and left Flynn feeling a bit flat. But then it happened – Flynn was nervous, but ready, and successfully passed his driving test four months after his 18th birthday.

His family could not have been prouder. To see Flynn reach a milestone in his life, at the same time as all his peers, was such an achievement. He is now a careful, calm P-plate driver on our roads and saved his own money to purchase his first car. Hats off to you, Flynn.

Zalie has also taken on the challenge of learning to drive in her stride. Her restricted learner's permit was lifted when she turned 17 years old, and from the girl who was too scared to leave the driveway in the car, she now loves cruising on a country road, driving to the local shops or through a McDonalds drive thru with myself or her driving instructor. With over 100 hours of driving behind her, I have total confidence that she will also reach the moment of passing the test to get her P-plates, and will be able to purchase a pink car, as she so desires.

On The Road

*It seems for success in science or art,
a dash of autism is essential.*

– Hans Asperger

CHAPTER 12

Where Can It Take You?

Zalie and Flynn are both naturally creative – they enjoy art, and art can tell a story. For Flynn, art is a hobby; for Zalie, art is a passion.

Flynn loves working with wood. He has made a side table, cabinet, coffee table and is now working on a desk. School wood tech classes progressing to product design classes have allowed him to explore this interest in his educational environment.

He has made some wonderful pieces of furniture which sit proudly displayed in our home. Flynn enjoys photography and drawing, subjects he is also studying at school and into VCE. Flynn, like Zalie, is a natural collector; he enjoys finding objects he can work on. During the fifth COVID-19 lockdown, in 2021, he returned from his afternoon walk with an old broken chair that he found by the river near our home.

It needed a new seat and the back repaired. Flynn got a piece of offcut timber from school and spent one Sunday afternoon repairing the chair. It has been wonderful to watch his patience and thinking skills progress and improve over the years. Another interest he has is in taking old tin cans, such as a Coke can, cutting them with tin snips and creating an aeroplane, for example.

Flynn is aware he has autism and speaks openly about it now at age 18. We told him when he was about 12 years old, at an age when we thought he was ready to absorb it. When he was younger, he was a lot more wired and busier. Now, he is very relaxed and has more of a sense about what he wants to do and what he enjoys. It really took a number of years for Flynn to understand that autism does not define him; it is a word that just describes a part of his personality. There are sometimes moments of self-doubt, when he may not quite understand a conversation amongst family or his peers. That it is also OK to interpret things differently to the majority, he also accepts. If you meet one person with autism, you've only met one. Autism is unique to each individual, different strengths, skills, personalities and coping mechanisms. Flynn understands his self-confidence is not as strong as he would like it to be and that social settings can sometimes be overwhelming. But over time he has learnt not to worry as much. In his early teens, he would get frustrated and a little angry at times, feeling like he didn't fit in.

But I tell him, even now, that it is OK to take a step back – if you are not sure what to say, you don't have to say anything. Just listen. Bring home what you hear and we can talk about it and I will explain it to you so you do understand. Then, the next time you hear it, or are in that situation, you will feel more confident.

This has been so important between him and I to have that connection – that he knows he can talk to me about anything and I will not judge; I will bring it back to black and white and always support him to be his best.

I know as Flynn moves towards finishing school and his future options, he would be best suited to utilise his creative thinking skills. He enjoys being outdoors. He volunteers every fortnight on a Sunday morning at a local community farm within walking distance of our home. He works in a team that care for the farm animals, this could include chickens, goats and lambs. They clean the pens and feed the animals. He has learnt to milk the goats and loves feeding the lambs and kids (baby goats) with bottles of milk.

Animals can sense the good in Flynn – if you can naturally connect with animals, it is a beautiful attribute to have. Flynn also enjoys the farm environment and interacting with local families who visit, often answering questions from them. Springtime is particularly special when all the baby animals are born.

Rarely a day that goes by where Zalie does not do some form of art. Starting at age seven when she first showed her artistic side, she preferred to create art to express feelings, emotions and thoughts, rather than talking.

At age 12, Zalie had her first major exhibition and art sale at La Trobe University through the Olga Tennison Autism Research Centre Annual Art Show. She was a young artist displaying her work amongst adults, sharing an evening with family and friends, enjoying drinks and canapes. It was very special, and a highlight when her artworks sold.

Zalie has also exhibited her work at the Melbourne Convention Centre, Montsalvat in Eltham, the National Gallery in Sydney, an International Autism Conference in India and many local places and venues including cafes, child-care centres, libraries, medical, sporting and recreational facilities.

Zalie has given her work for fundraising events with Autism Actually and the Pat Cronin Foundation. Now, at age 18, with her own art studio at home, Zalie can actually call herself an artist.

She has been part of many solo and group exhibitions and has sold over 30 pieces of her own work. Predominantly working with acrylic paint and mixed media on canvas, Zalie also creates clay sculptures, makes her own jewellery and loves to draw, particularly woman and clothing designs. She has her own distinctive style, completely self-taught, which is always cheery, bright and happy – just like her really.

In 2019, Zalie's art, along with other autistic artists from around the world, was published in a book put together in the United

Where Can It Take You?

States, titled *Art Without Boundaries: Living on the Spectrum* which can be purchased online through Lulu Publishing. Zalie connects her art with people through her own Facebook and Instagram page and also with other autistic artists through The Art of Autism, a non-profit international collaboration of talented individuals who come together and display the creative abilities of people on the autism spectrum and others who are neurodivergent. Zalie loves exhibiting and sharing her art with people. Her work hangs in many private homes and offices, as well as public places. Zalie always display a profile alongside her art and people love to read her story – a journey that has thrown at her many challenges, but she continues to grow.

I have always been the voice for Zalie's art, contacting people and venues, such as local cafes or libraries, to ask if they would display her work by hanging it on their walls. It is not a job I am trained for, being an art advocate, but if I don't do it for Zalie, then who will? I feel we have made some great progress so far and hope one day someone else steps in and sees her potential. Zalie always gets compliments on her work and it gives her the inspiration to continue.

When Zalie draws now, her people tend to have faces; she has become very skilled at drawing a beautiful, animated face, accentuating the eyes and giving definition to the mouth. However, when she paints there is a mix – sometimes there are no faces and she instead focuses more on movement and body position, as even the simple movement of the way hair falls around a face can tell a story. As Zalie is an excellent observer – she takes in more than you would assume. She has a natural ability to sculpt and draw body proportions and has done so from a very young age.

At this stage, Zalie's art studio is a downstairs space in our home. I have visions of a larger standalone studio for her with big windows to let in lots of natural light and with plenty of display and storage space sometime in the future.

Zalie has grown into a kind, considerate, attractive young woman. Communication is still her biggest barrier, but every day she surprises me with how these skills are still developing. She still works on her ability to engage in conversation and people find her pleasant and polite. At age 16, it was her time to finally grasp the concept of team sport, now playing in an all-abilities netball team. Zalie's highlight this year has been participating in her Year 12 Presentation Ball. With all the restrictions due to COVID lockdowns it was wonderful to see this special moment actually go ahead for her. As a mum, it was beautiful to see her all dressed up, and her request was to share her special persons dance for the evening with Flynn. I think Flynn had just as much fun as Zalie that night, enjoying a lot of dancing and fun on the floor.

Bryce, Anaye, Zalie, Flynn

As Zalie and Flynn approach the end of their final year of secondary school, I am proud to say they both have a lot of potential. We have made it this far and they have some amazing accomplishments behind them. The thought of making decisions with and for them at the end of one journey and the start of a new one post-school is somewhat daunting – maybe exciting, but definitely scary. There is a real mix of emotions. I don't think anyone really knows at age 18 exactly what they want to do with their life. It is harder for parents of students who require additional support, as we wear the weight on our shoulders more to help them make those decisions.

I would like to thank everyone who has played a role in Zalie and Flynn's journey so far. They would not be where they are now without the support from some very special people during each stage from toddler to teenager. As they progress into adulthood and take on different pathways, I know their stories will continue. My support for them and thoughts of their future are with me day and night. As mums of amazing individuals who have faced their challenges, we do sleep less and worry more, but our magical moments are just that much more special as only we know how hard it was to get there.

Take care and you may hear from me again in the next phase.

Zalie's art has been displayed and sold in the following locations:

Montmorency Secondary College
Our Lady Help of Christians, Eltham
Café Zen Den, Eltham
Eltham South Fine Art Gallery
La Trobe University, Bundoora
Melbourne Convention Centre
Volumes Café & Giftshop
Northpark Private Hospital
Hoyts Cinemas
Dynamic Vegies and Café
Earthbound Bolton Café
Eltham Library
Diamond Valley Library
International Autism Conference, India
Belle Art Start 2020, National Gallery, Sydney
Smile Council Orthodontics, Bundoora
Cooper Butterfly Hair Salon, Eltham

Where Can It Take You?

The Edge Performers School
Smart Speech, Research
Montsalvat, Eltham
Miss Pryors Café, Eltham
Chocolate Lily Café, Eltham

Thank you to everyone for supporting Zalie and her art.

About the Author

Joanne Elaine is a mother of four living in a leafy suburb of Melbourne, Australia.

After completing Year 12 at school, Joanne worked in many varied and interesting industries for over 20 years as an executive assistant and auditor, transitioning to part-time when she became a mum. Returning to study at RMIT (Royal Melbourne Institute of Technology) when her youngest child was two years old, Joanne then worked with children with disabilities at pre-school and primary schools while juggling her busy home life.

Joanne enjoyed writing poetry when she was younger and has always been an avid reader. Her dream of writing a book has evolved over several years with a hope to share her journey, experience and knowledge with others.

Joanne has an interest in public speaking and has been on school committees, coached and managed netball and basketball teams, volunteered at the school canteen and is always there to support her children.

Footsteps of Two is Joanne's first book, an honest and heartfelt insight from a mother of twins on the autism spectrum. A story of navigating unknown territory and finding inner strength.

With a strong interest in healthy eating, exercise, home renovating and travel, Joanne's outlook on life is one of never giving up, which has assisted her to support her twins with their greatest challenges.

Mother to Bryce, Zalie, Flynn and Anaye, Joanne has enjoyed making her dream into a reality by finishing this book. She hopes to share her positive personal story to help others navigate a similar journey.

Notes